THE BOX BOOK

THE BOX BOOK
The World's Cheapest Way to Build Furniture

WRITTEN & ILLUSTRATED BY
DIANE CLEAVER

David McKay Company, Inc. · New York

To
Walter Mathews
who taught me everything I know

and
Mary Cherry
who has a cupboard full

THE BOX BOOK

COPYRIGHT © 1974 BY DIANE CLEAVER

All rights reserved, including the right to reproduce this book, or parts thereof, in any form, except for the inclusion of brief quotations in a review.

LIBRARY OF CONGRESS CATALOG CARD NUMBER: 73–84064
ISBN: 0–679–50417–6
MANUFACTURED IN THE UNITED STATES OF AMERICA

Acknowledgments

Several friends helped, with assorted boxes, advice, assistance, and blatant amusement and, for different reasons, I'd like to thank them: Allison Heisch, Jim and Toshi Parsons, Robert Hobbs, Joann Johnson, Larry Ashmead, Catherine Hopkins, Philip Spitzer, and David Krotz.

Acknowledgments

Several friends helped, with assorted boxes, advice, assistance, and blatant amusement and, for different reasons, I'd like to thank them: Allison Heisch, Jim and Toshi Parsons, Robert Hobbs, Joann Johnson, Larry Ashmead, Catherine Hopkins, Philip Spitzer, and David Krotz.

Contents

Introduction	xi
Some Boxes to Look For	1
Tools: Very Few	5
Lumber and Other Things You'll Need	11
Space: Some Ways to Save It	19
Things to Build and How	27
The Totem	27
Cupboards	35
A Wall Unit	39
The Cabinet	41
A Digression	46
The Wall Unit Again	48
Drawers	51
Finishing the Wall Unit	54
Couches and Other Things to Sit On	56
Chairs	60
Seat Covers and How to Make Them	71
Bookshelves	74
Tables	81

CONTENTS

Children and Boxes	91
Pure Folly	95
Some Odds and Ends and Decorative Things	101
Finishing Things Off	109
Index	113

AND NOW I began to apply myself to make such necessary things as I found I most wanted, particularly a chair and a table; for without these I was not able to enjoy the few comforts I had in the world; I could not write or eat, or do several things, with so much pleasure without a table.

So I went to work; and here I must needs observe that as reason is the substance and original of the mathematics, so by stating and squaring everything by reason, and by making the most rational judgment of things, every man may be in time master of every mechanic art. I had never handled a tool in my life, and yet in time, by labour, application, and contrivance, I found at last that I wanted nothing but I could have made it, especially if I had had tools.

DANIEL DEFOE, *Robinson Crusoe*

Introduction

*What you cannot as you would achieve,
You must perforce accomplish as you may*
SHAKESPEARE, *Titus Andronicus*

CONGRATULATIONS! YOU'VE FOUND an apartment, you've paid the first month's rent, a month's deposit, the agent—and you're broke. But you'll save money on a moving van. With several friends you can move your books, records, and clothes. When you get some money together you will buy a bed and secondhand furniture. In the meantime a mattress on the floor will be fine, and you'll unpack later.

That moment when you're first alone in your very own, totally bare apartment is delicious. The plain, empty spaces seem like endless plains of fresh air. There's room to move, to live an uncluttered, uncomplicated life. Furniture seems unnecessary, an intrusion. But floors get hard, and fantasies extend to include a comfortable chair for reading, a chest of drawers so that you can find your underwear, shelves on which to put your books and records. And such things usually require an investment of money.

The solution to furnishing your apartment attractively, inexpensively and with originality lies in boxes—wooden boxes that can be found anywhere in the country. Boxes that have been used to carry fruit, milk, liquor, appliances, all kinds of things from one end of America to the other, and across oceans. They come in different shapes, different sizes, different qualities of wood, and they can all be transformed into furniture, furniture that is pleasing, fresh, and easily built.

Unlike any other "do-it-yourself" effort, a box is already in a usable form. It can be a container, chair, bookcase, or table. It depends entirely on how and where it stands and what you decide you want it to be. It's a microcosm of your apartment—a container, empty, bare; it needs some work and it needs your imagination to make it unique, to make it more than a container or box. You are no more limited in deciding what it will be than in deciding to make your apartment French Provincial, Early American, or just a place where you're comfortable and at home. You don't need much money to do it and you can't buy it in any store. Before lifting or hammering a nail you can fill your apartment with boxes and call it furnished. With very little money and a few tools, you can transform your boxes into real furniture, comfortable furniture that will be unique in character and much better looking than anything you're likely to obtain from friends, relatives, secondhand stores, or the Salvation Army.

There is absolutely nothing more depressing than having very little money and being forced to hunt for secondhand furniture. It's secondhand, because it's beat up, broken, ugly, or totally useless. If you do find furniture that's "possible," it needs endless scrubbing, scraping, sanding, mending and, finishing. If you're lucky, it ends up being bearable—at least for a while. It is possible to come across real "finds" (grab them), but they're rare. It's almost always safe to assume that the seller knows exactly what he's doing—he isn't giving anything away.

It has taken me fifteen apartments, nine years with hardly any money to spend on any of them, and furniture garnered from every conceivably honest course open to me, to discover boxes. This, my latest apartment, is filled with boxes.

There are grape boxes from Greece, plum and milk crates from New Jersey, orange boxes from California, Drambuie boxes from Scotland, and exotic boxes from Hong Kong and Taiwan. They are square, slatted, and rectangular. They serve as cupboards, chests, tables, stools, and storage areas. My only concession to mass manufacturing is a bed, and if I'd thought of it before, it'd be made out of boxes, too.

Wooden boxes are found on the streets, in fruit and vegetable stores, in supermarkets and liquor stores. Liquor boxes are harder to come by, but befriend your local liquor man, buy a bottle occasionally, and you, too, will acquire some fine boxes. Good wood is used to make liquor boxes; they're more finely made, and they're usually white and clean. The strongest boxes are wooden milk crates. They're reinforced with metal strips around the edges. Bleecker Street in New York is a gold mine of boxes. It's lined with fruit and vegetable stores which show their produce on street stands. After closing hours, the boxes are piled high along the side of the road waiting for the garbage collection. Though outside New York City, street boxes will be harder to come by, most cities have neighborhoods similar to Bleecker Street or weekly outdoor markets, and they're well worth visiting, because here you'll find the largest, and most accessible, source of boxes. Chinatown in any city is invaluable. Chinese boxes are usually well made and sturdy, there's great variety in size and shape, and the Chinese lettering adds a touch of the exotic. Supermarkets and liquor stores take a little cultivation, but it's worth it, and in smaller towns they are perhaps the only reliable source for boxes.

The complement to boxes is plywood. It comes in any size, several thicknesses, and different grades. If it's finished properly, it looks good. I've used plywood for the coffee table top (which is so finely finished I claim it looks like mahogany), two chairs (the design copied, more or less, from expensive chairs in a department store and which is passed on here, page 61), and a bookcase that had to be fitted into a narrow space.

Building your apartment out of boxes and plywood is an investment of time, not money. Expenditure is devoted to stains, shellac, enamel paint, brushes, a few nails, and tools. Comfort is added with liberal use of foam rubber which can be bought in any shape or size, and fabrics to cover the foam rubber.

Once you start collecting boxes, it becomes a fetish. I find myself looking at everything along the street that appears to be a throwaway. If I like a shape or color or grain of a piece of wood or metal, I pick it up and use it somewhere. Friends save their junk for me. Copper tubing from a plumbing job is now a lamp stand, a piece of textured plastic backs one of the boxes, tiles are for standing hot dishes on, and a piece of floor is a paperweight. And there's this long wooden leg that I'm trying to find some use for. Everything is disposable for somebody; others of us watch out for it and pick it up with glee. Keep your eyes open for renovation sites; good pieces of wood are often thrown away.

INTRODUCTION

In the course of this book I shall be making some assumptions. First, that your apartment is something like mine—small; second, that you want to furnish it as comfortably as possible for a minimum expenditure and that you're prepared to spend a little time doing it; and third, that you don't want to acquire lots of belongings that tie you down when you want to move on. A great advantage to boxes, to making furniture from them, is that it doesn't seem like work. They have endless uses and variations, and you'll find endless ways of incorporating them into your apartment.

I enjoy my apartment and hope to pass on some ideas that you can use, too. At all times, the concerns are how to spend as little money as possible, how to make pieces of furniture comfortable and attractive, and how to utilize space to its best advantage.

Boxes are symbols of many things—Freud and dreams, gifts, Depression-like poverty, economy. (Thorsten Veblen, the economist and author of *The Theory of the Leisure Class*, used boxes to furnish his apartment.) A box is a pure form; you can make it into anything.

Some Boxes to Look For

And all Arabia breathes from yonder box
POPE, *The Rape of the Lock*

THERE ARE ALL kinds of wooden boxes to be found; practically everything is shipped everywhere in them. Wooden milk crates abound in New York, but they might be hard to find in California or Milwaukee, because they use plastic ones. It doesn't matter—as long as the box is made of wood, it can be transformed into furniture; whether it was originally used to carry milk or wine is unimportant.

Boxes can be found all over the place—garbage dumps, the backs of supermarkets, on the streets waiting for garbage pickup. Most everything is shipped somewhere—food, clothes, equipment, furniture—and a lot of it is shipped in wooden boxes.

Orange crate

Orange crates aren't used just for oranges, they're just called that. They carry cantaloupes, grapefruits, pomegranates, and other fruit. The typical orange crate is 24" x 13" x 13". Rather than being solid wood, it's slatted and, like most boxes, is made from box wood. It's not as strong as a solid wooden box, but the slats give it a particular appeal, and it is strong enough to be used for a table or to stack books in.

1

Milk crate

Although they're changing to metal or plastic crates, milk companies are still, to a large extent, using wooden boxes. Milk crates are the sturdiest around, and I've used them as the basis for several pieces of furniture. They're made from solid wood panels and have metal runners around the edges (which can be taken off if you like), and measure $12\frac{1}{2}"$ x $16\frac{1}{2}"$ x $10\frac{1}{2}"$. They're also returnable. The milk company delivers the fresh milk and picks up their crates from a previous delivery. They don't seem to be very strict about this, and you can pick milk crates up outside most supermarket and grocery stores. If they're not left around outside the store, the manager of the supermarket will probably give them to you.

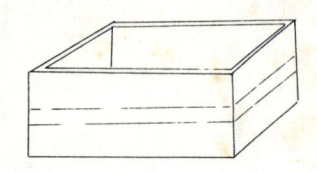

Plum crate

They're small ($17"$ x $16"$ x $4\frac{1}{2}"$), light, flimsy and not much good for making furniture, but they are ideal for hanging in bathrooms and kitchens. With shelves inside, they're perfect for spice bottles, pill boxes, jars, and what have you.

SOME BOXES
TO LOOK FOR

Drambuie and wine crates

There was a time when all liquor and wine was shipped in wood boxes, but that's becoming fairly rare. Some wine companies, though, still ship their goods in wood boxes rather than the cardboard ones you want when you're moving. Christmas is a good time to find wood liquor boxes, however. You should ask your local liquor store to save any wood boxes for you; it's worth the time to collect them, because they're usually in very good condition. Sizes depend very much on the manufacturer and the size and shape of his bottles, but an average size is $18\frac{1}{2}''$ x $16''$ x $9\frac{1}{2}''$.

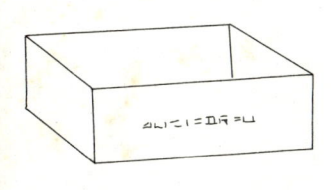

Grape box

One of my favorite boxes is a grape box from Greece ($11\frac{1}{2}''$ x $13\frac{1}{2}''$ x $12\frac{1}{4}''$). It's the only one I've seen, but I keep checking the local greengrocers. I use it as a footstool. It's slatted and has feet which raise it slightly above the floor. It's actually very similar to the boxes used for carrying bottles of purified water. They're not easy boxes to pick up, but maybe you have purified water delivered. If you can get one, they're strong and can be made to look really good.

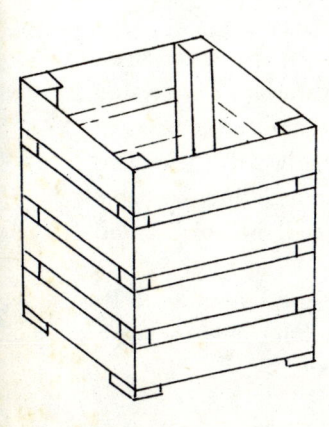

Tea chest

If you live in or near a city, there must be a coffee, tea, and spice store nearby. Tea is shipped from Europe, generally England, where it's processed, in large wooden tea chests. They measure 23″ x 20″ x 15″ and are perfect for making cabinets and chests. They also smell good. It's worth making a trip to a tea store to get hold of one; if you don't pick them up, they'll just be thrown away.

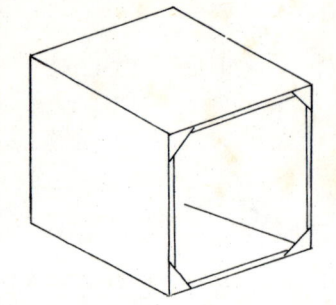

Chinese boxes

Boxes from China, or rather Hong Kong and Taiwan at the moment, come in all shapes and sizes, are usually very well made, sometimes exquisitely, and are easily available on the sidewalks of any Chinatown. They're used to ship abalone, bean sprouts, Chinese vegetables, rice, just about anything that goes into a Chinese meal. It's usually more difficult to find a cardboard box in Chinatown than it is to find a wooden one. They also have Chinese lettering on their sides, which somehow has more style than "New Jersey" or "Florida" in plain old Phoenician lettering.

All kinds of furniture is shipped in wooden crates, too. You can find out delivery dates and times at a local furniture store, and when the goods are unpacked you can take over the crates. Some of them are far too large to use as they are, but the wood is good and can be sawed to different sizes and used to make such things as table tops and cabinet doors. Some of the crates will be smaller and usable as they are.

If you aren't interested in finding boxes, and can afford to be totally decadent, there are now orange crate kits for sale; they cost about $7 and come with nails, boards, and labels.

Tools: Very Few

This Hitteth the naile on the hed
JOHN HEYWOOD, *Proverbs*

I HAVE NEVER read any kind of repair manual that did not say you should use good quality tools. This is fair enough, but operating on a minimum budget doesn't allow for good quality tools; they are expensive. One advantage might be that they last longer, and they are things you'll always need, but my inexpensive tools are holding up very well. My hammer, for example, cost 85 cents, and there hasn't been one job that it hasn't been up to. The head's still on the handle, and the handle isn't cracking or peeling. I can't, in fact, imagine how it's possible to destroy this hammer.

You will need very few tools to build your whole apartment. As you design and build more furniture you will, in spite of early good intentions not to spend money, become quite interested in, and sophisticated about, tools. Hardware stores have a tremendous fascination—they're full of wonderful gadgets you have rarely, if ever, known of; gadgets and tools which spark off all sorts of new building, repair, and refining techniques. For an extremely good beginning, though, the Five-and-Ten has all the tools you need. You won't be doing any fine or complicated cabinet work (at least not yet), so the simplest, most basic tools will be all that you'll need.

They are:

Hammer

This is the first thing you think of, because you probably won't want to hang your pictures in the same places as the previous tenant, and it is essential for pulling old nails out of the walls (or, if you can't pull them out, knocking them in). The hammer you buy shouldn't be too lightweight. You'll need something with a little muscle, in the 12 to 16 oz. range. The head should be the gently rounded claw type, which drives in nails and pulls them out with the minimum of damage. If you try to pull a nail out of a plaster wall without taking the following precaution, you will bring part of the wall away with it. Before hammering in the nail, place a small piece of masking or Scotch tape on the wall and knock the nail through that and on into the wall. This way, if you have to pull the nail out, the plaster will stay up and you'll have only a tiny hole where the nail went in. You can buy a hammer with either a wooden or fiberglass handle. The only advantage to fiberglass is that it doesn't alter size with changes in humidity, as a wooden-handled hammer does. A wooden handle somehow feels better, but it can sometimes shrink and loosen from the head.

Drill

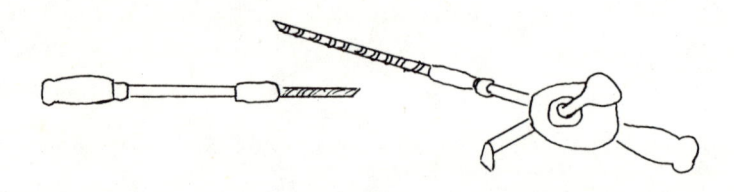

This is a marvellous piece of equipment. There are various types, but basically what you want is a simple drill to drill holes. You will need holes for endless things—anchor screws (for hollow walls), holes for screws, nuts, and bolts. The basic Five-and-Ten drill works on a bouncing motion. You tap a slight indentation into the wood with nail and hammer. You will need the dent created by the nail on which to place the head of the drill so that it doesn't slide around. You then pump the drill up and down with one hand and without any effort the hole is there. There are also drills with handles which are turned to create the same pumping effect. Drills come with different size heads; mine has four diameter sizes. If you should need a hole larger than half an inch, you will need a brace and bit; but you probably won't.

Screwdriver

There are probably more types and styles of screwdriver than any other tool on the market; you'll need one with interchangeable heads. Until I discovered boxes, I had no idea that screwdrivers weren't all flat at the tip. Eventually, I came across a screw with a rounded head criss-crossed on top in which to fit the head of the appropriate blade; I needed a Phillips-type screwdriver for this. They come in sizes 1 to 4. Most Phillips screws will require a Number 2 head, so you can still make do with one screwdriver. Mine has four heads, three of different flat widths and a Number 2 Phillips head. The most convenient length for a screwdriver is 4″ to 6″.

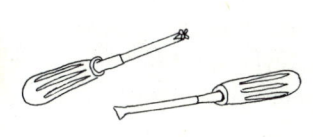

Pliers

These will have what is called a slip-joint, which means that it has two notches and can be adjusted to fit things that might need gripping—such as a nut. You should buy a pair that has a cutting edge for wire. They are also very useful for adjusting hooks if you bought the wrong size and for getting screw caps off bottles that won't screw. It's a gripping tool, and you'll have endless uses for it.

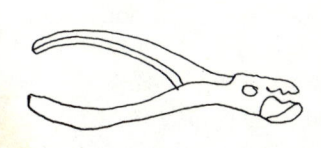

Scraper

This is for scraping down anything—walls with falling plaster, boxes encased with dirt and paint spots from the floor.

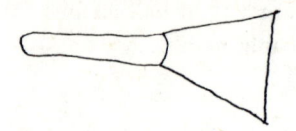

Saw

This is absolutely necessary and again something which comes in endless variations. A 20" hand saw is large or small enough for any sawing job you're likely to encounter. It should be a cross-cut blade to cut against the grain of the wood. It's unlikely that you'll have to cut lengthwise into any piece of wood, so you won't need a ripsaw. After marking wood to the right length, start sawing on the waste side (that is, the end of the wood you won't be using) of your line; otherwise, you'll probably end up slightly short. After sawing through the wood and finding yourself a bit long, it's easy enough to use a rough piece of sandpaper wrapped around a block of wood to take off the edge. Incidentally, you'll need lots of sandpaper too.

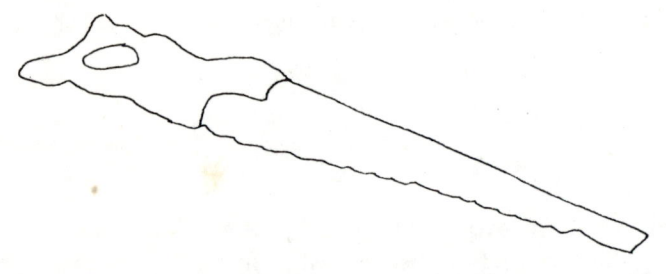

In addition to these tools, you will of course need lots of nails and screws. Buy variety packets of nails in hundreds. The most useful length in screws will be $\frac{1}{2}$" for small jobs and $1\frac{1}{4}$" for larger work. These two sizes will see you through most things. Actually, you won't be using that many screws and nails; an effective alternative is Epoxy glue, contact cement, or possibly nothing more than the support of boxes and plywood on each other. You will not need the Epoxy glue that requires two tubes (resin and hardener);

the one-tube type will be more than strong enough. The only slight drawback to glue is that furniture will not be so readily taken apart. But it is possible—it just takes a little more time.

One other thing you'll need is a tape measure (or rule). If you get a measure, buy the metal kind that rolls into its case when you press the button on the side of it. A 6′ rule is actually easier to use; it's a little more expensive, but worth it.

These suggestions for a basic tool kit would shock a good handyman or carpenter. It is true that you can't do a good job without good tools, but that means the right tools not the expensive ones. The tools I've listed are basic to any carpentry kit. Their uses are flexible, and if a pair of pliers will unscrew a bottle cap, it is the right tool. Your carpentry work might not be the smoothest in the world at first, but I guarantee that when you've finished building your apartment no one's going to know you didn't use the right technique or the proper tools.

Lumber and Other Things You'll Need

> Only a sweet and virtuous soul,
> Like seasoned timber never gives
> GEORGE HERBERT, *Virtue*

THERE ARE MANY different kinds of woods, beautiful lumber, but to make the things this book describes, information about all of them isn't necessary. For our purposes, you need to know about . . .

Plywood

It comes in several grades and different thicknesses. It can be used to build practically anything, and should be used because it's cheap and, if finished properly, can look almost as fine as any other wood. It comes in panels measuring $4' \times 8'$ and in standard thicknesses of $\frac{1}{4}''$, $\frac{3}{8}''$, $\frac{1}{2}''$, $\frac{5}{8}''$, and $\frac{3}{4}''$. Each side of a panel is graded separately, ranging from A to D. If you're building a table, the top of it should be graded A—you don't want lots of holes and cracks to show. It doesn't matter about the bottom side; no one's going to see it, and grade D is fine. As long as something doesn't show, you don't have to worry about grades—the wood itself is just as strong.

It's worth figuring out, before you go to the lumberyard, just how much of the $4' \times 8'$ panel of plywood you'll be using for any project. If you're like me and can't figure this out easily, cut a pattern of the object out of newspaper first and play around with it, fitting the pieces in a $4' \times 8'$ area. If the project requires less than a $4' \times 8'$ panel, you'll be charged for the whole piece, in which case you should ask the lumberman for any scrap pieces. If what you're ordering is half of the total panel ($4' \times 4'$) or less, you will be charged for only half.

Plywood is made from several thin layers of wood which have been glued and pressed together. It's stronger and less likely to warp than regular lumber. It does, though, have rough edges, and furniture can be finished off by gluing or tacking molding along it's edges.

Pine

This is the cheapest wood to use for large areas of bookcases. Standard bookshelf sizes are $1'' \times 9''$ and $1'' \times 12''$. Because of the drying process through which the wood goes, a $1'' \times 9''$ is not what it says; it's actually $\frac{3}{4}'' \times 8\frac{5}{8}''$.

All lumber is graded, and pine is no exception. It's graded 1 to 5, the smoothest, best graded, being #1. For bookshelves, knotty pine is fine (#2 or #3). The knots, for the most part, won't show, and if they do you can fill any cracks with wood putty.

Moldings

It is sold in strips by footage and in several widths. $\frac{1}{4}''$ to $1\frac{1}{4}''$ is usual, although wider molding is available. Smaller lumberyards carry only flat ("Butt") or rounded molding, but larger yards and some hardware stores also stock it with various designs imposed on the facing side. Molding is a fraction of an inch thick, flexible, easy to use, and can turn a roughly finished piece of furniture into something that looks professionally finished.

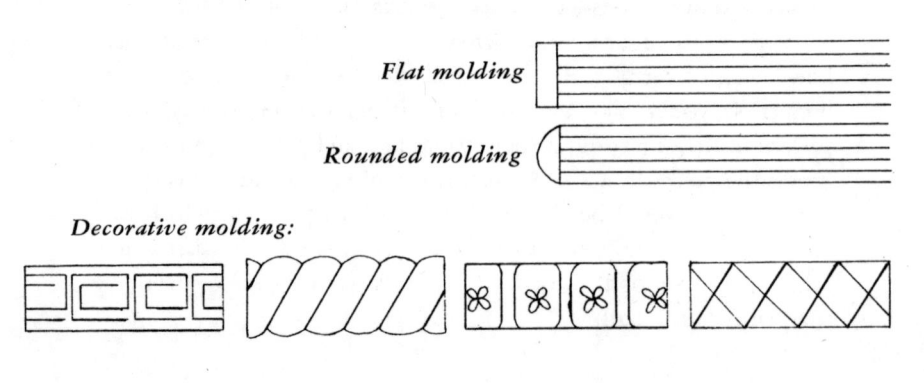

Flat molding

Rounded molding

Decorative molding:

Hardboard

You won't use this often, but it is good for building drawer bottoms, dividers for records in cabinets, pigeonholes in desks, or ends of cabinets which won't be exposed. It can be sawed and nailed just as if it were solid lumber. It generally comes with one smooth side and one rough side. The smooth side is easy to paint, the other isn't, so it should be used with that in mind.

All lumberyards have a scrap barrel full of odd pieces of wood, left over from various orders and too small to sell, which are thrown away unless people take them. The lumberyard will be delighted that you want the odd pieces. If you don't see the throwaway barrel, ask, and it'll be pointed out to you. Some lumberyards don't collect the odds and ends of wood until the end of the day, or at a particular time each day. If you check with them they'll give you the time, and you can get first pickings. You'll find that you're always needing odd pieces of wood for different things—shelf supports, or to build a base. Lumberyard scraps are an invaluable free source.

Nails

There are several types of nails, the difference having to do with their purpose and whether or not you want them to show on the finished work.

Because boxes and plywood don't allow for "fine" cabinet work, it doesn't matter too much whether you use common or finishing nails. To be precise, though, finishing nails are set slightly beneath the surface of the wood and should be used for cabinet work or whenever you don't want the heads of the nails to show. Common nails differ only in head size—they're broader, flatter, sit flush with the surface of the wood, and are visible.

Brads are just like finishing nails except that they're smaller and thinner and used for lighter work, such as attaching molding to the edges of plywood tables and chairs, or fixing $\frac{1}{4}''$ plywood to the back of a bookcase.

When nailing one piece of wood to another, select a nail

length which is about $\frac{1}{4}''$ less than the combined thickness of the two pieces. If you're nailing a thin piece of wood to a thicker one, drive the nail through the thin piece first and on into the thicker piece.

To drive finishing nails beneath the surface of the wood, take a blunt nail, place the sharper end of it on top of the head of the finishing nail which is almost flush with the wood and hammer it below the surface. The slight indentation left by the nail's entry is filled with wood cement. When the surface is finished, the nail should be difficult if not impossible, to see.

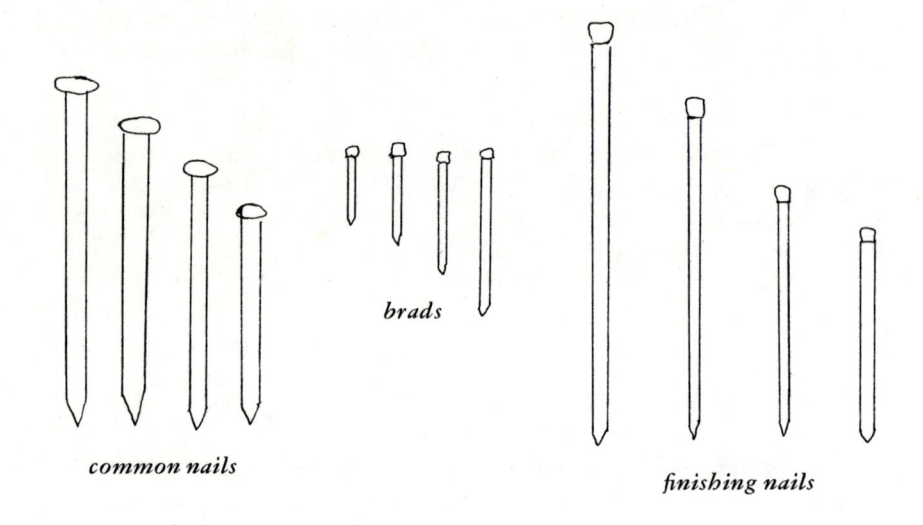

common nails

brads

finishing nails

Screws

The most convenient and useful is the flat-headed screw, although they also come with round or oval-shaped heads. Phillips head screws also come flat, round, and oval but they're not as easy to use, and there's no reason that I know of to do so.

Screws are used primarily for attaching fixtures, doors to

**LUMBER
AND OTHER
THINGS
YOU'LL NEED**

cabinets, hinges, bookshelf supports—the finishing touch type of thing. Before putting one into a piece of wood you should drill a small pilot hole into the wood. This will make the actual screw-driving easier.

As with nails, they come in many sizes and thicknesses. Sometimes round or oval-headed screws are used decoratively, and they are made from brass, chrome and other metals. Whether or not you use them depends on whether you want them to show and be part of your design.

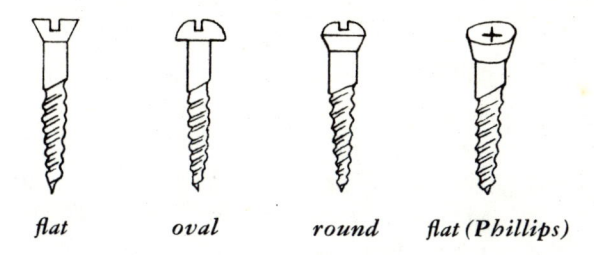

flat   *oval*   *round*   *flat (Phillips)*

Braces

Braces are used to support things—a shelf, a small cupboard, or even large bookcases. The two kinds used for support purposes in this book are basically the same, although the one on the left in the illustration, the smaller, squared-off one, is the kind you can use to hold a bookcase against a wall or to strengthen the corners of a bookcase that doesn't have the backing that would otherwise give it strength. The brace on the right comes in several sizes and can be used for putting up the odd shelf.

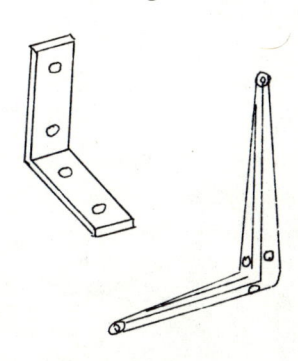

15

Hinges

There are all kinds of hinges: functional and/or decorative. They are made from brass and a variety of other metals. I like brass hinges, so most of the cabinets I've made show them off.

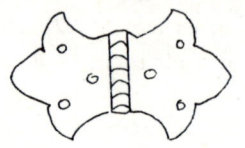

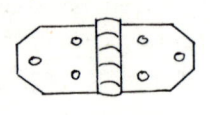

If the edge of any box/cabinet is too narrow (and sometimes they are) to take a hinge which shows (or if you don't like brass hinges) you can use plain old steel and hide them, the only part showing being the center joint.

There is also something called a piano hinge; it comes in 6' strips which can be cut to size. It's used where lots of support is needed—on a table which folds up into a bookcase, for example. Holes are placed every $2\frac{1}{4}''$ for screws.

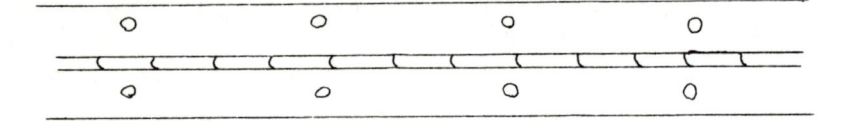

Fixtures

Door handles, knobs, and drawer pulls come in wrought iron, brass, porcelain, and practically everything else. There are many styles, and function will often determine what you buy. Go to any good hardware store and ask to see such fixtures; often they'll be prominently displayed. It's a good idea to check them out before you begin building; it'll give you an idea of the options.

LUMBER AND OTHER THINGS YOU'LL NEED

Legs

Standard lengths are 3", 6", 9", 12", 15", 18", 22", 29". Styles vary, and although not cheap, they can be worth the expense. They can make a mundane piece of furniture fun and different. Legs shouldn't be thought of as just legs. They can be used in the body of a cabinet—caryatid-like—and you can create arches and corners and all manner of fantasy.

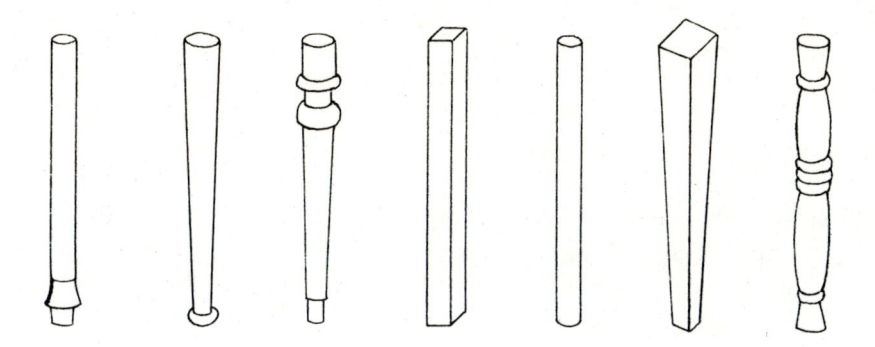

Glue

Contact cement is the best thing I've found. Elmer's Heavygrip isn't made for enormous gluing projects, but it's the only thing I've used for any of the light pieces I've built. It's really an aid to assist in the nailing of woods together, not something to depend on for total support. You put glue on the two surfaces which are to be joined together, allow the pieces to make contact, pull them apart to let the air in (which somehow adds a quality of strength), and place them together again. The two pieces won't always hold immediately—if they're on a vertical for example they'll slide apart. Use a piece of masking or Scotch tape to hold them in place. For stronger support use Epoxy glue.

Wood putty

is invaluable. Although it comes in cans and tubes, the tubes are easier to handle. Fill the crack with wood putty, let it dry, sand it down flush with the surface of the wood, and when it's painted or stained the crack or hole or knot won't show at all.

Space: Some Ways to Save It

> I think no virtue goes with size
> RALPH WALDO EMERSON, *The Titmouse*

MOST OF THE apartments I've lived in have been fairly small; they've been studios and at the most had a small bedroom. My current kitchen is actually on the edge of the living room, but a bookcase has cut it off, making it a separate room, a galley. It doesn't seem to matter how many rooms there are; more space is always needed. And closets are at a premium. In spite of best intentions, things accumulate.

In building my apartment I've tried to maintain a maximum freedom of movement in the space there is. I don't like clutter, and I don't like heavily furnished dark rooms. I want space, and if I'm in a 3′ closet I want it to look and feel like a 6′ closet. It's an odd thing, too, that an empty room will look smaller than a room with something in it. Even one chair very often makes the difference in the feeling of space. Everything in my apartment is, in a way, built-in, designed for movement and accessibility. Rather than being space-saving, it's space-expanding. It's being built with hit-and-miss methods; some storage cupboards became useless, because doors opened the wrong way, and I'd have to think again, or sometimes I'd find that shelves could be used to better advantage. But gradually it's working out, and hopefully it will keep improving, always becoming more convenient, more comfortable, more spacious.

Boxes are movable and constantly changeable. They have an added advantage over other furniture, too, when you're ready to move again you won't need to collect cartons from supermarkets or liquor stores—you just dismantle your furniture, use it to pack your belongings, move, and reassemble it in your new apartment in different ways if you choose.

Because my own kitchen is so small (6′ x 3′), and is located at the entrance to the apartment, it was a good place to start building. The most obvious space-saving method is hanging things—not just utensils and pots, but box-cupboards to hold all kinds of small things that can clutter a kitchen.

One of the dedicated aims of most city apartment dwellers is the defeat of the cockroach. They say that if you don't leave food around, dirty dishes, staples in paper packages in cabinets, or leave a messy stove, the cockroaches won't find anything to eat and will go to your messy neighbor's apartment. This is not entirely true—they also like wood, linen, Saran-wrap, and aluminum foil. However, we tend to believe Them, and with this dictum in mind I keep all staples, such as flour, sugar, cookies, croutons, and tea stored away in saved coffee cans. Perhaps some of the cockroaches are foiled—at least they don't have an open invitation to drop by. (Actually, the only sure-fire way to get rid of cockroaches is to paint. They hate it.) Anyway, coffee cans invariably take up more room in the cabinets than the usual paper packaging and crowd out dishes and cutlery.

SPACE:
SOME WAYS
TO SAVE IT

This brings us to the first box. Mine's a wine box 20" x 13" x 6½", which is a convenient size to put in two shelves and hang on the door. On the shelves are nine brightly painted coffee cans (the color theme is blue and orange) which house my staples.

The shelves in this coffee-can cabinet are made from two end pieces of another wine box. (Always, by the way, collect more boxes than you think you're going to need for any particular project; they can be broken down and the wood used for bases, supports, and shelves.) Shelves are nailed into the box from the outside. Turn the box on its side, nail them in from one side, turn the box over, and nail firmly into place. To get the exact size of the shelves needed, measure from the *inside* base of the top or bottom of the box. Be careful not to splinter the wood when nailing in the shelves, use slender 1½" nails for the best results.

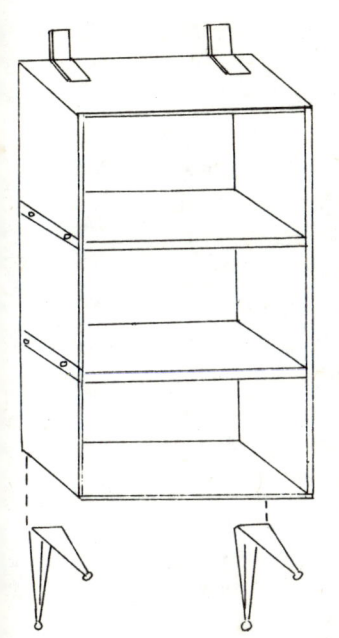

Braces are used to support the box, small ones at the top, larger ones at the bottom. I find it easier to put the braces on first and then attach the whole thing to the door or wall. The braces will take four screws each. Make sure the supporting sides of the brackets, underneath the box (the shorter sides) don't reach the edge of the box—give them half an inch at least.

When the braces are attached to the box, hold it to the door; the braces should be flush with the box and meet the door evenly. Before screwing the box in you should decide where the bottom of it should reach and make screw holes for it. With a pre-started hole you should be able to handle the box and its brackets and put in the screws. Don't use screws longer than ¼", if you're putting the box on to a door (which is probably hollow); they'll be too long and won't hold. When the braces are fully screwed into the door or wall, it's firm, but not firm enough. You should put two more screws through the back of the

21

box and into the door. Again, the screws shouldn't be long—just enough to go through the box and into the door.

If you can't find pieces of wood from another box that are about $\frac{1}{2}''$ thick from which to make shelves you'll need to tack in some shelf supports to rest the shelves on. Any odd strip of wood will do for this as long as it's at least $\frac{1}{2}''$ square, strong enough to hold the shelf and be backed solidly into the box. The supports are tacked into the box at the height where you want to rest the shelves; the shelves are tacked to the supports.

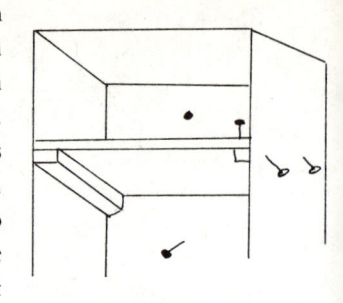

With a galley-like kitchen there's no room for a trash bin unless you don't mind walking around it, kicking it over, or doing without one. My solution to the garbage pail problem was to hang it on the back of the door, underneath the coffee-can cabinet. I must admit to not having used a wooden box in this instance; I was only hanging things in those days, not boxing them. With a plastic garbage pail about 16" x 13" x 9", I used the same system as described in the coffee-can cabinet—two braces and six screws, and in this case, two hooks. It's stayed up through tons of garbage. A wooden box of the right dimensions for your needs is even better; that can be fixed to the door or wall in the same way as the cabinet.

Actually, you'll need only four screws if you use a plastic garbage pail. You can't screw the base of it to the braces, you can only rest it on them. This time, put the braces into the door first. Put the pail on top of them and see where it falls. I made two holes in the top of the pail, put two screws through the holes, and into the door. They're square-ended screws, about $\frac{1}{4}''$ of screw and perfect for a hollow door. The two hooks and the support of the braces will be fairly strong and should support all the garbage you've got to dispose of. If the hooks or the screws seem to lack firmness in the hollow doors, put a drop of "glue anything" cement around the screw. It'll give added strength.

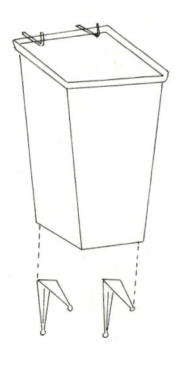

SPACE:
SOME WAYS
TO SAVE IT

Although necessity required me to use the door (see sketch below), cabinets and, of course, trash pails of any shape or size (or boxes), can be used on walls, too.
I painted the braces, which attach and show on the door, the same color white, as the door. I stained the coffee-can cabinet: I have a thing about stained rather than painted wood. Even if it's cheap wood, it still looks good if it's finished properly.

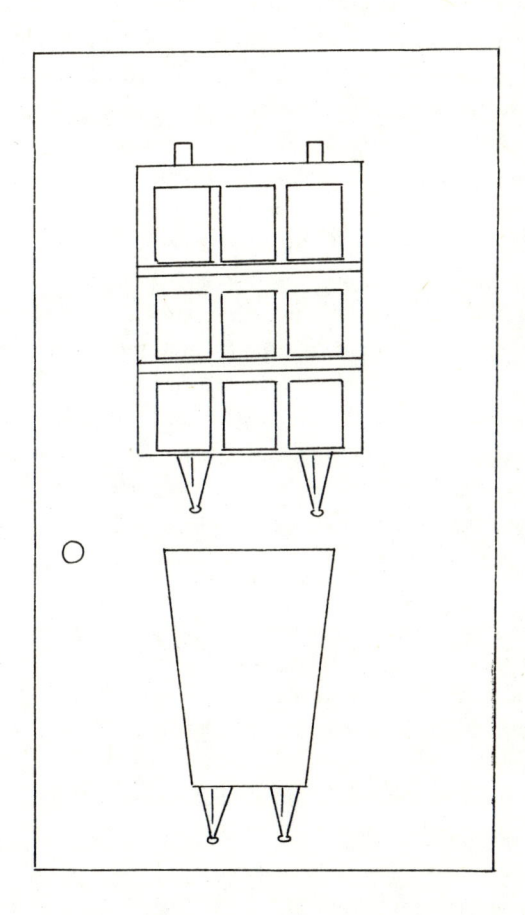

Other convenient kitchen things are: a piece of pegboard, which we all know about. (It's good to hang pots and pans and a shelf for spices.) A plum crate is ideal for a spice rack; it's narrow enough to hold the spice bottles without losing them and you can

23

fit half a dozen shelves into it and, if you like to use lots of spices, have lots of spices on hand. If you want a wine rack, hang it above a door out of the way; my continually empty wine rack is, of course, *above* the kitchen door. Although not always easy to reach (I have to stand on a box), everything's out of the way, and I can work in my galley without falling over everything, or losing it all.

There's never enough room in the bathroom either. There are always too many bottles of medicine, cosmetics, and perfumes. A plum crate can be useful here, too. Put in a couple of shelves and you can immediately fill it with bottles that won't fit in the medicine cabinet any more. (Be sure of the size of your bottles before you begin; it's very easy to fix a couple of shelves into a box and then discover that all your bottles are just an eighth of an inch taller than the shelf space you've allowed.) You won't need the heavier boxes in the bathroom, although if there's room for them, there's no reason why not. The plum crates are lighter and a little easier to hang. Tack in two double-pointed tacks, one on each side of the upright box, two hooks or small nails into the wall and just hang the box on them. It will need support, but the large braces aren't necessary—two small ones are fine. Even a couple of long, heavy nails, knocked into the wall directly under the base of the new cabinet will give it all the support it needs.

The plum crate is ideal for the bathroom. It's only $4\frac{1}{2}''$ deep and ideal for bottles of shampoo and pill boxes. Use either tacks or picture hooks on which to hang it. At the bottom use either two sturdy nails or preferably two small braces.

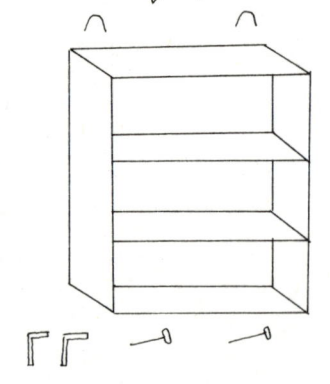

There is always a need for extra shelves, and the bathroom, because it's small, lends itself to very easy installation. Lumber comes in various standard sizes (see pp. 11–12), and one of them

SPACE:
SOME WAYS
TO SAVE IT

is just right for a bathroom shelf. Get a plank of 12″ (x whatever length you're covering) x $\frac{1}{2}$″ thick of either plywood or knotty pine. Place one end on top of the door frame and run the other end to the opposite wall on which you will already have fitted a metal brace or a strip of wood for support. When measuring the length of your shelf from wall to wall, measure at the height the shelf will be placed. I have measured for just such shelves at my own convenient standing height only to discover that they wouldn't fit. Walls, it seems, are never squared, they're narrower or wider at the top or the bottom. It's only a slight difference, but a $\frac{1}{4}$″ or $\frac{1}{2}$″ is a big difference when you come to fitting shelves in precise areas.

Without nails or supports, you can fit a shelf on the wall side of your bathtub. The tiles, which generally only go up three parts of the wall, can be used to place the plank on. If you've got a narrow bathtub, it won't work, because you'll keep hitting it when you're trying to shower. Measurements here must be very precise, because there's not much room to balance the shelf on the tiles.

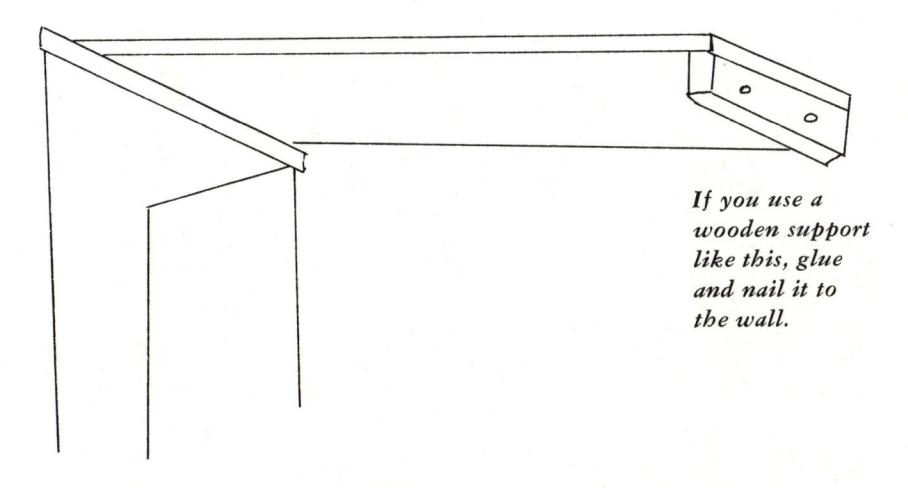

If you use a wooden support like this, glue and nail it to the wall.

These cabinets and shelves should be painted or stained while they're still boxes and planks of wood. They'll look neater, and there won't be any awkward corners you can't reach. The later

25

sections on finishing and decorative effects give the information for professional touches that will make your cabinets a real "finished" piece of furniture.

When putting up the shelves in the bathroom, remember that you'll only be seeing the bottom of the shelf. If you decide to use knotty pine planking, put the knots on top, where no one can see them.

Space can be expanded in many ways—it's mostly an illusion—and I'll keep referring to it through this book.

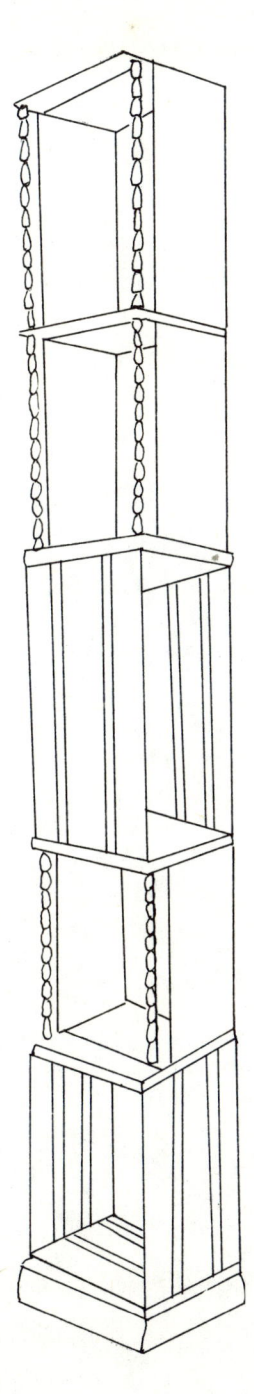

Things to Build and How

*A little further, to make thee a room
Thou art a monument without a tomb*
BEN JONSON, *To The Memory of
My Beloved Author William Shakespeare*

THIS IS A TOTEM. It was the first thing I built, because I needed storage space for books and papers in a working area. I thought, at first, in traditional terms of buying a cabinet—too expensive; or stackable, wooden storage boxes that some department stores sell—too expensive. My immediate problem was solved when I suddenly began to notice that I was walking past dozens of wooden boxes on my way home every night. I started picking them up, carrying them home, and stacking them in my bedroom until I could decide exactly what to do with them. Never, by the way, pick up a box that has been used to carry fish. Endless scrubbing doesn't take away the smell, and it's not worth the discomfort or bother. All the boxes need washing down, some of them scrubbing. Do it in the bathtub. If you decide to paint or stain them, this should be done now. It's convenient and fairly quick to do it as you collect the boxes, rather than waiting until you've accumulated a whole bunch—at least it's less tedious, and you can get on with building sooner. The section on finishing, page 109, gives all the information you need to be able to do this.

Although I'm describing some of the pieces I've built, you shouldn't feel confined by them. The furniture here fits my apartment. I hope the ideas will be taken as suggestions, as possible adaptations into the space you have to work with, to your needs, to your apartment. This particular totem is in the corner of the room. To build it you will need:

1) Three orange crates, 24" high x 13" deep x 13" wide. Take apart one of the orange crates, which will give you nine strips of wood measuring 3" x 24" and two base sections 13" x 13" x 1" high.
2) Three milk crates, 16½" high x 10½" deep x 13" wide.
3) Six wooden legs 16½" long.
4) Ten wood screws, some brads, and a small metal bracket.

1) To build the base of the totem to the height of the wall baseboard, take the two 13" squares and nail them together. To make it even higher (to meet with the height of the baseboard), nail three strips of wood cut from the 24" long x 3" wide strips from the spare orange crate across the top. This will give you a smooth platform exactly the height of the baseboard on which to build upward with the boxes. Your baseboard might be higher or lower; use the spare wood from the "spare" box in any combination to create a height equal to the baseboard. Even if your wall doesn't have a baseboard, a platform on which to build the totem gives security and strength to the structure. It also looks better.

You'll have nine of these struts; you'll need to cut them into smaller strips. Don't throw bits and pieces of wood away; there's always a use for them

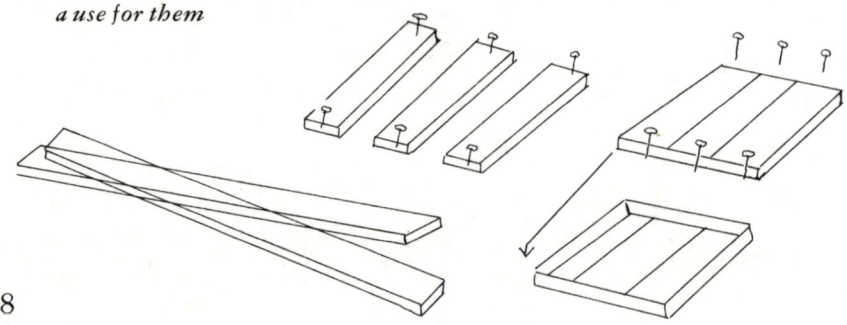

2) Place the base of the totem flush against the base of the wall, don't nail it to the floor; it'll be just fine. The weight of the boxes plus the final brace attached to the wall will hold it very steady. The first box, an orange crate, goes on top of the base. It can either be flush against the walls or given $\frac{1}{2}''$ breathing space on its two wall sides. The base gives this flexibility. If the first box is placed on the floor without a base you will be prohibited by the baseboard from placing the totem boxes flush against the walls. Use one screw to attach the bottom of the orange crate to the totem base.

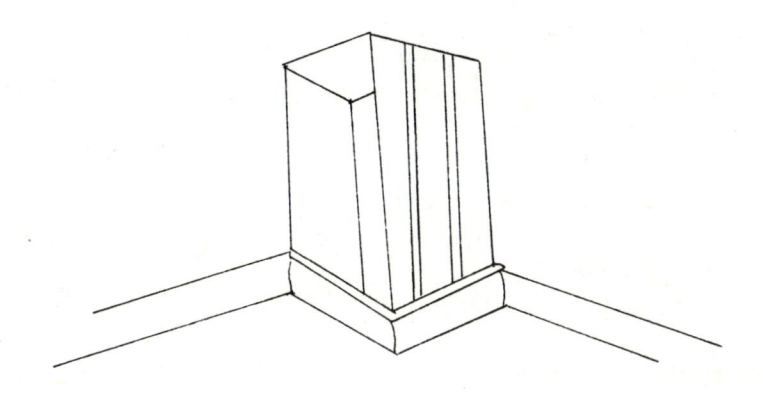

3) The second box is a milk crate which is $2\frac{1}{2}''$ shallower than the orange crate. Place it on top of the crate so that the backs and sides of both boxes are flush with each other. Attach the boxes together with a screw through the bottom of the milk crate into the top of the orange crate.

4) The third box is another orange crate. Place it even with the back and sides of the milk crate (it'll overhang by $2\frac{1}{2}''$) and screw the two boxes together.

Be flexible in putting the boxes together—they don't all have to face the same way. (They don't all have to be milk crates and orange crates either. Any sturdy boxes will work.) This totem is five boxes high, four of them face in the same direction, and one of them, the third box, faces directly into the room. I liked the slats of the orange crate and wanted to show them off. There are no books or papers in this box—it holds a lamp and a trailing philodendron. I like the lamp, the plant, and the shadows they create when the larger room lights are off. A practical piece of furniture shouldn't be all practical; it looks more complete, more cared for, with some space for something which allows a different texture.

Because the orange crates are $13''$ square, it was quite easy to face this one in another direction.

The second box, the milk crate, is now fixed between two orange crates. It is shallower by $2\frac{1}{2}''$. Balance is brought to the structure by wedging legs ($16\frac{1}{2}''$ long, the same height as the milk crate) between the top of the first crate and the bottom of the third. The legs are in front of the milk crate and look as if they support the top orange crate.

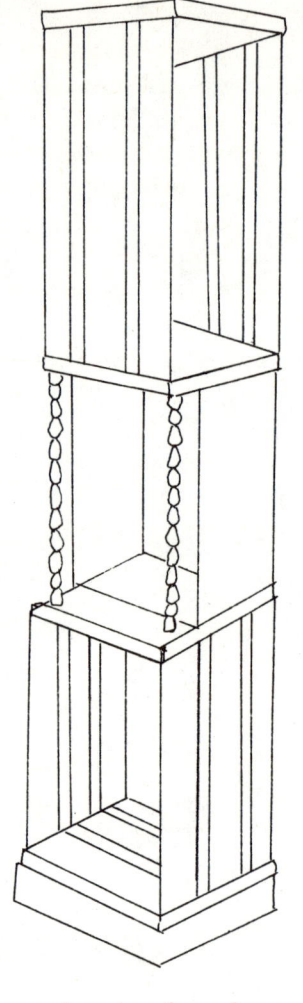

I bought the legs at a hardware store, but any lengths of wood will do; you can even cut a broom handle down to the proper lengths.

5) The fourth box is another milk crate, again $2\frac{1}{2}''$ narrower than the orange crate beneath it. Place the milk crate on top of the orange crate so that the sides and back of both boxes are flush with each other. Screw them together. Because my ceiling wasn't high enough to take another orange crate of $24''$ in height, the fifth box on the totem is also a milk crate, only $16\frac{1}{2}''$ high. So that it would all even out, I accommodated the $2\frac{1}{2}''$ left by the shallower milk crates by building a hood (or overhang) from the top of the milk crate and putting legs in position to bring it all together.

The milk crate is $16\frac{1}{2}''$ high; the legs should be the same length. They need hoods of $2\frac{1}{2}''$ to match up with the front of the orange crates on which they're resting. Again, use a strip of wood

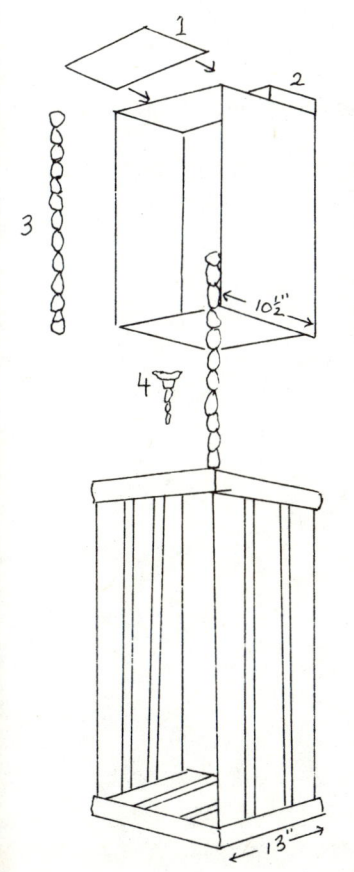

The overhang (1), if you use the orange crate strut, is 3" wide. The extra ½" is tacked to the top of the milk crate. The other strip (2) is tacked to the back of the milk crate to bring it even with the front.

The legs have been cut to 16½" high and are wedged into place. They should be quite firm, but you can put an extra tack in from the top (3).

You'll need one screw, put in from the base of the milk crate through the top of the orange crate (4).

You can add any combination of boxes to those already established in precisely the same manner.

from the crate you took apart earlier. Cut two pieces 13" wide from the 3" strips. One piece is tacked to the front of the box, $\frac{1}{2}$" actually into the top of the box; the remaining $2\frac{1}{2}$" create the hood. The second piece of 13" x 3" wood is attached to the back of the box to make the surface even with the front. Cut the legs (or broom handle) to the exact length of the milk crate (you want them to fit tightly, so cut on the far side of your saw line) and wedge them between the top of the orange crate (the third box up) and the overhang you've created on the milk crate.

6) The fifth box is also a milk crate. Place it on top of the fourth box (milk crate) and join them together with *two* screws, one at the front, through the bottom of the box, the $\frac{1}{2}$" of overhang, and into the milk crate on which it's attached. The second screw goes at the back of the box through the bottom of it, the piece of wood between, and the milk crate underneath. Put a hood on the top of this box, too, and wedge the legs into position between the hoods of the two top milk crates.

7) The whole structure is held to the wall by one bracket (see diagram below). It's a simple thing which takes four screws, two into the wall and two into the top of the top box. The whole structure is now perfectly steady and balanced.

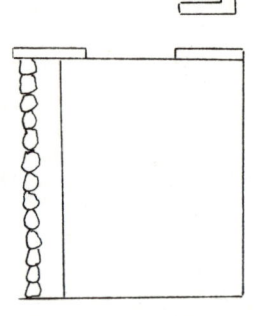

In building the totem I didn't want to just stack a bunch of boxes, I wanted to build something that looked good, like furniture. The boxes I chose to use were of two different sizes. Using all milk crates seemed cumbersome, all orange crates too flimsy. With a combination of the two, the totem worked out to be very stable, but at the same time it has room to breathe, it doesn't crowd the corner or dominate anything else. In using boxes of different sizes, you have to worry about accommodating them to each other. You don't want the structure to be awkward, and they should balance and complement each other. You may not be using orange crates and milk crates to build your totem, but the same principles apply.

If you don't want to use legs to balance the whole it can be done another way. The orange crate, for example, is $2\frac{1}{2}''$ wider on one side than the milk crates. Rather than accommodating the difference by using legs, the discrepancy in size could be accounted for by adding a $2\frac{1}{2}''$ strip of wood between the back of the milk crates and the wall. A strip of wood from the broken-up orange crate could be cut to the right dimensions; this would be glued or wedged between the back of the milk crate and the wall.

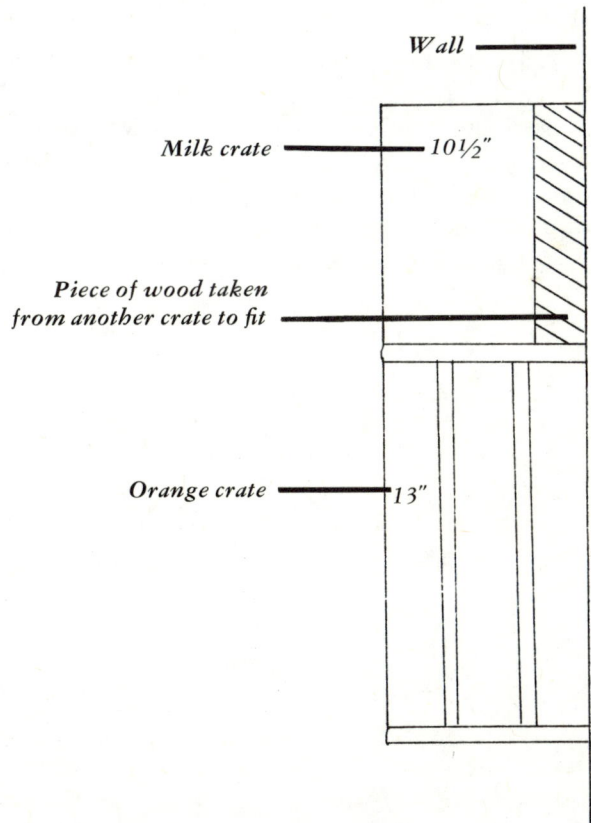

Wall

Milk crate — $10\frac{1}{2}''$

Piece of wood taken from another crate to fit

Orange crate — 13"

As I mentioned before, this was the first thing I built, ever. It took several hours of staining, sawing, and hammering away one Thanksgiving. I was very pleased with myself. I should perhaps mention that it was only part of a whole wall unit. The second half took even longer and involved a screen 9′6″ high x 6′ wide. I won't bother with more details, because it didn't work. I did get the whole thing up, but even I couldn't admire it. It took me a week of walking past it to acknowledge its failure and another half an hour to take it down. My point is that you're going to use time to produce some failures, and it's painful recognizing them. But you can experiment, without committing too much of yourself, with boxes, and much of it will be encouraging; you'll keep building, get a feel for sizes, how things will look before you touch a nail, and the failures will disappear. The totem is pretty straightforward to begin with.

There's no particular reason why the totem has to be in the corner of a room. It could just as easily be placed in the center of it, to break up space, create corners, and offer access to its cupboards from different sides. Shelves and doors can be attached. Two or three columns can be built, lined up, placed back to back, in a square, work as a room divider, cupboards for all your belongings made out of it. It can be as low or tall as you want it.

Cupboards

> But what can Miss E[...]
> Want with a [...]
> So long, narrow and shal[...]
> And without any l[...]
> WALTER DE LA MARE, *Peeping T[...]*

TO MAKE A cupboard take a box

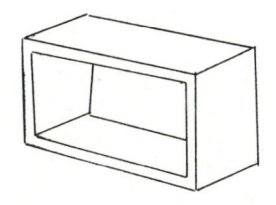

Attach one or two pieces of $\frac{1}{2}''$ plywood, cut to exact size, to its edges with hinges:

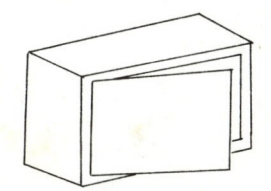

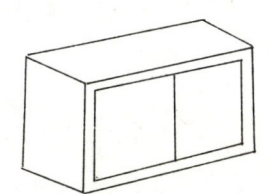

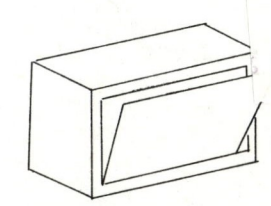

With legs, or a base, knobs, handles, and drop-fronts or doors, it becomes not only useful but decorative:

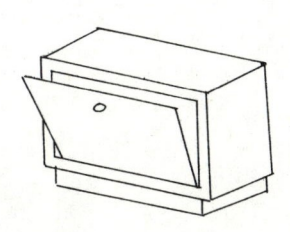

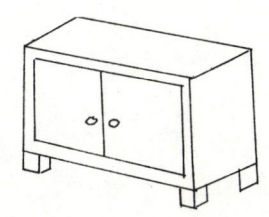

Put two or four or five boxes together and they become a unit which can be the beginning of a wall of bookshelves, cupboards and storage space, a room divider, or a foot locker:

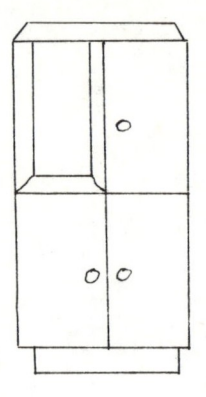

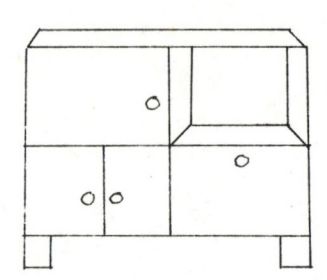

To be sure you get the door cut to the right size, measure the *inside* dimensions of the box; the door will fit at the front inside edges. Reduce these measurements by $\frac{1}{4}''$ on the vertical and the same on the horizontal. If the inside dimensions of the milk crate, for example, measure $15'' \times 12''$, the door dimensions should be $14\frac{3}{4}'' \times 11\frac{3}{4}''$. If you don't allow this space, the door won't fit, or move easily, when it is attached with hinges.

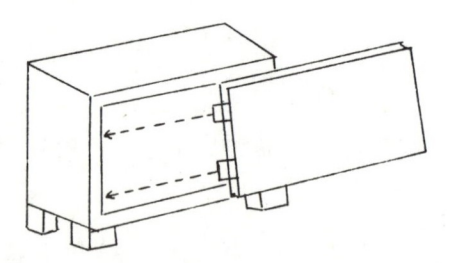

Legs are easy to fit (they come with screw heads), but the base can be a little more complicated. You'll need 1 x 2s or 1 x 3s to make the base. (A 1 x 2 is a piece of lumber which measures $\frac{5}{8}''$ thick x $1\frac{5}{8}''$ high; A 1 x 3 is $\frac{5}{8}''$ thick x $2\frac{5}{8}''$ high. You'll note that 1 x 2 or 1 x 3 doesn't mean anything. The lumber used to have those measurements, but has since dried out and shrunk.) Basically, what you will be doing is putting a frame underneath the box, raising it from the floor. A base like this is good for practically any kind of cabinet, chest or cupboard. If it's a particularly large piece, you can add crossbars for additional strength:

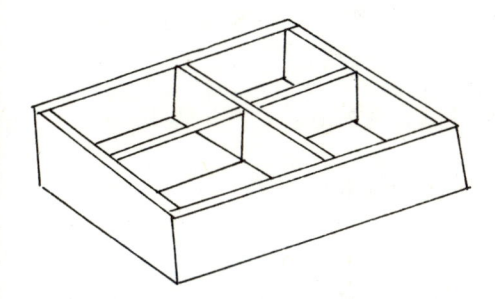

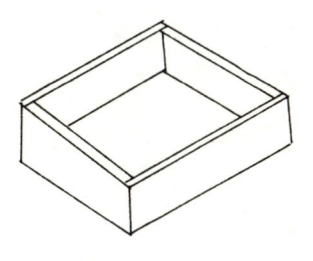

The base is mostly decorative, although it does raise the structure from the floor, keeping it free of dust and easier to keep clean.

The outside dimensions of the base of the milk crate are $12\frac{1}{2}''$ x $16\frac{1}{2}''$. The base dimensions are $12'' \times 16\frac{1}{2}''$. The *sides* of the base will be $\frac{1}{2}''$ shorter than the sides of the milk crate to create a slight indentation at the front of the crate/cabinet and to show it off. To show a clean line at the front of the cabinet, the side pieces of the base should be nailed between the front and back pieces:

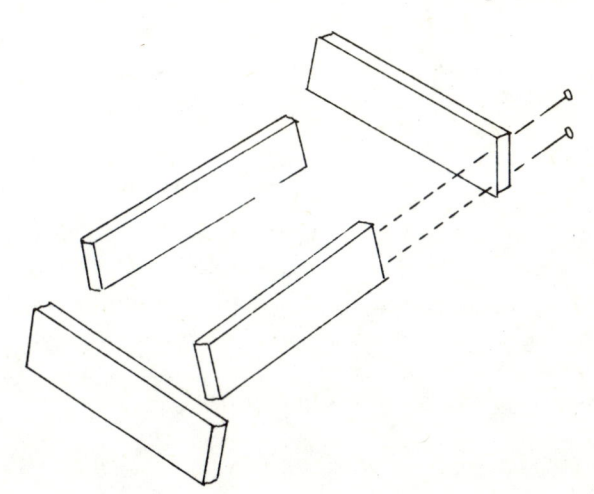

Measurements can be tricky, and misjudging by even $\frac{1}{16}''$ can, at times—such as when fitting doors, shelves, and bases for cabinets—be disastrous. The time spent figuring it all out precisely before you go to the lumberyard is worth all the extra work it can save you.

The outside measurements of the milk crate are $12\frac{1}{2}$ x $16\frac{1}{2}$, the outside dimensions of the support base $12''$ x $16\frac{1}{2}''$. These are not the lengths of wood you order. You must deduct the thickness of the front base (on a 1 x 2 or 1 x 3, it's $\frac{5}{8}''$) from the length of the side pieces of the base. On this milk crate base, the front and back pieces are cut to the width of the box—$16\frac{1}{2}''$; the side pieces are cut to $10\frac{3}{4}''$.

On this milk crate base, the front and back pieces are cut to the width of the box, $16\frac{1}{2}''$, the side pieces are cut to $10\frac{3}{4}''$. The sides pieces will be nailed between the front and back pieces; $10\frac{3}{4}''$ allows for the indentation at the front of $\frac{1}{2}''$ and the thickness of both the front and back pieces of the base which is $1\frac{1}{4}''$ altogether. You don't have to be precise about $\frac{1}{8}$s of inches. It's easier to go to the nearest $\frac{1}{2}$ inch. It doesn't matter if the front indentation is slightly less than $\frac{1}{2}''$ or slightly more, it's just a visual thing anyway.

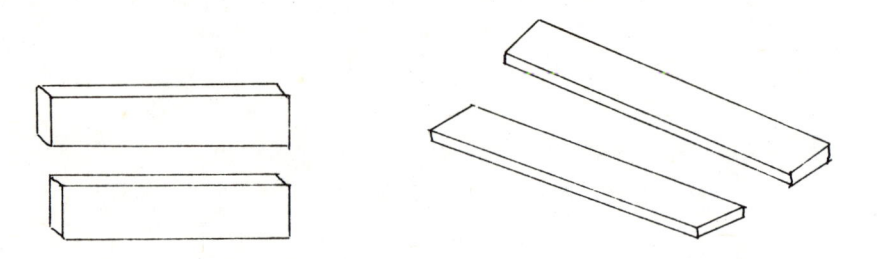

My first venture into door fitting and base building took me twice as long as it should have. I didn't think about the dimensions properly and I didn't think about the thickness of the wood having to be accounted for somewhere. Trying to cut the odd $\frac{1}{2}''$ off a length of wood is ridiculous; it's a waste of time, and you can never cut the edge as straight as the lumberyard can.

THINGS
TO BUILD
AND HOW

A Wall Unit

> I beheld the wretch—the
> miserable monster whom I had created
> MARY WOLLSTONECRAFT SHELLEY, *Frankenstein*

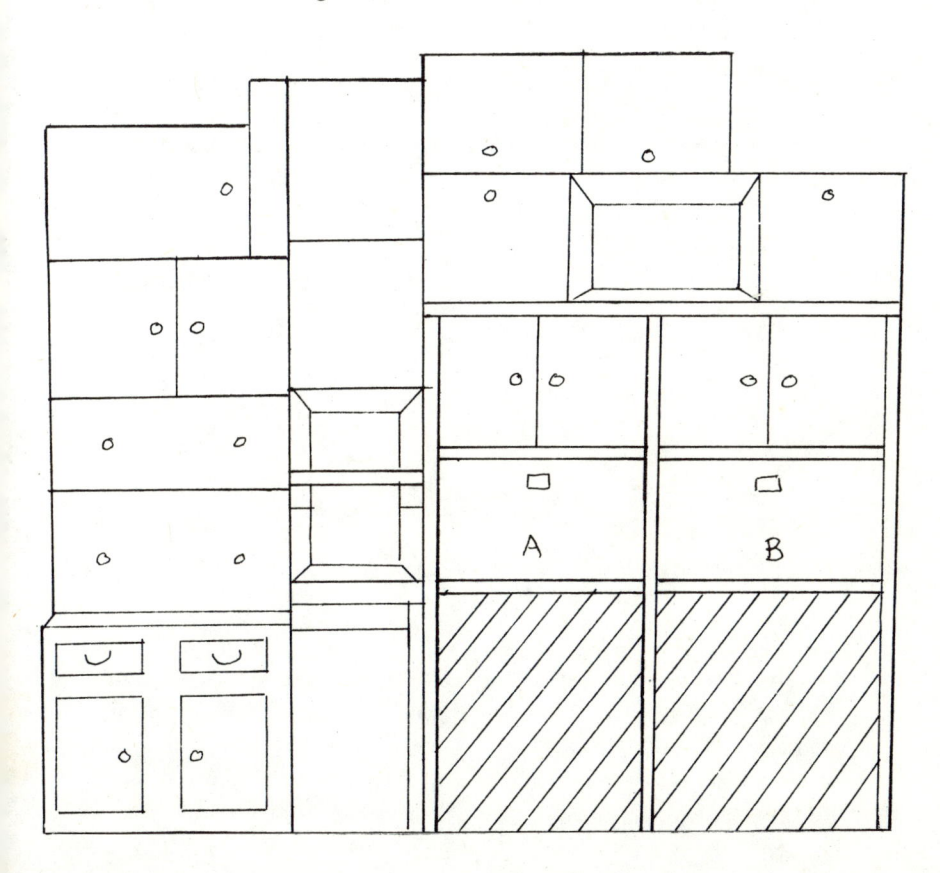

Apartments never have enough storage space, and they're often too small to accommodate chests and wardrobes, which might absorb some of the excess. I'm always surprised at the amount of garbage I carry out of my apartment every day. And it's nothing compared to the amount of stuff I save every day. My storage problem resulted in this elaborate, somewhat monstrous, but easy to build, structure I have in my bedroom which measures about 11′ high by 6′9″ wide. Part of it became the headboard to the bed, and all of it is useful and accessible for storage. It's a combination of eleven boxes, an old chest and a cupboard I built from an old shelf, 2 x 2s, plywood and hardboard.

The shaded area is behind the bed. The cupboards A and B are the headboard. The space behind the bed, 9" of it, was useless before it was built into this cabinet. The whole structure works for me. Your storage problems are probably different, but there might be some suggestions here which you can incorporate into your own design.

With 9" space behind the head of the bed and the wall, boxes as storage wouldn't have worked. They would have been inaccessible and a waste of space. This whole structure breaks down into units, and they are adaptable for different uses in different rooms.

For the whole unit (although remember you might use eight boxes or fifteen instead of eleven, and you might not have an old chest), I gathered together the following things:

1) Eleven boxes of varying styles and sizes: six milk crates, one wine crate, and three boxes from Chinatown, each of different size.
2) One old chest
3) Six 2 x 2s, 54" high ⎤
4) Two 2 x 2s, 52" long ⎬ These are all lengths, but "high," "long," and "wide" indicate their placement in the construction
5) Two 2 x 2s, 6" wide ⎦
6) One plank of wood (knotty pine) 52" x 9"
7) Two pieces of hardboard 54" x 9"
8) Two panels of $\frac{1}{2}$" plywood 23" x 23"
9) Panels of $\frac{1}{2}$" plywood cut to the various door and shelf sizes
10) Sundry nails and glue

It sounds like a lot, but it isn't too bad, and it all goes together. The list does indicate, though, that you have to think carefully about the structure as a whole before you launch into it. Thinking about it beforehand could save you some trips to the lumberyard.

THINGS
TO BUILD
AND HOW

The Cabinet

Much as I try, I have to admit that boxes don't always work. This cabinet was built around an old piece of shelving I found on the street. I cut it down to 52" in length and used it as the base around which to build the cabinet or headboard. I decided to use the shelf as the starting point, because I had no idea exactly how I was going to build this cabinet, and I thought it would be something solid to work from. Another of my problems was working at the back of the bed in 9" of space—maneuvering was a problem.

I found the right height for the headboard by sitting on the bed in my usual reading position, marking where my head came to on the wall ($35\frac{1}{2}"$) and adding an extra 4" of height in case I wanted to sit up straighter. It came to $39\frac{1}{2}"$ in all. As the real reason for building the cabinet in the first place was a strong center for all these boxes I had piled up, I added an extra $14\frac{1}{2}"$ for security. The total height of the cabinet is 54". It's a firm, useful, convenient base.

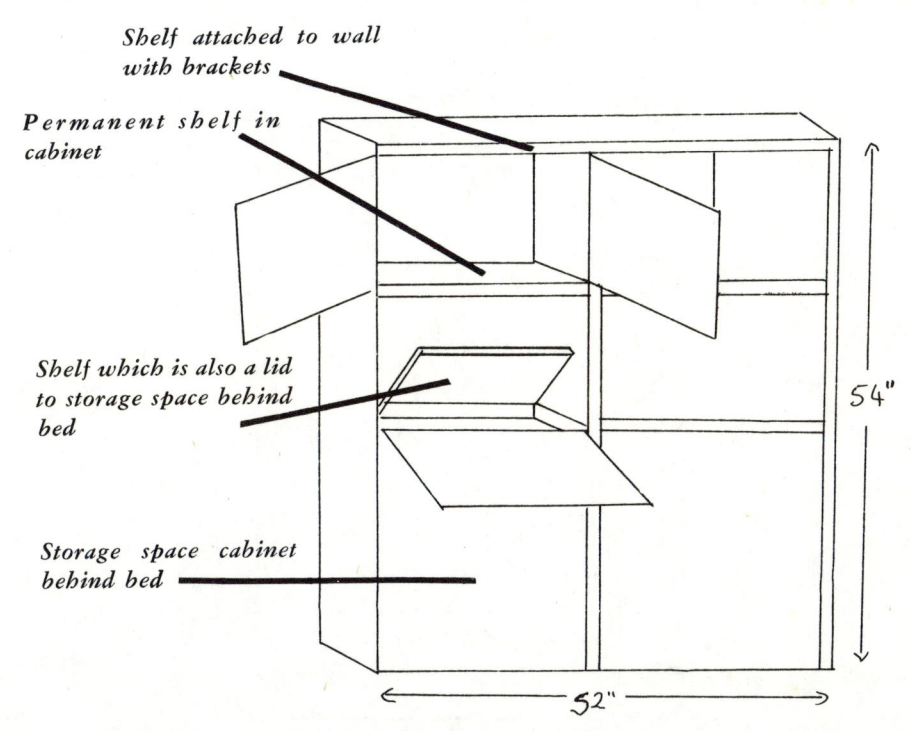

Shelf attached to wall with brackets

Permanent shelf in cabinet

Shelf which is also a lid to storage space behind bed

Storage space cabinet behind bed

54"

52"

41

THE BOX
BOOK

1) Attach the 52" x 9" shelf to the wall with 6" brackets.

2) Make a base from four pieces of 2 x 2s; two at 52" and two at 6", nailing the shorter pieces between the longer ones. The outside dimensions of the base should be the same as the shelf, 52" x 9".

3) Because the shelf's already attached to the wall, it's somewhat easier to handle the frame supports. Attach the 54" long supports with 2" nails driven through the top of the shelf into the top of the supports. The bottom of the supports are attached to the base by glue, which is applied before the nails are knocked in from the top.

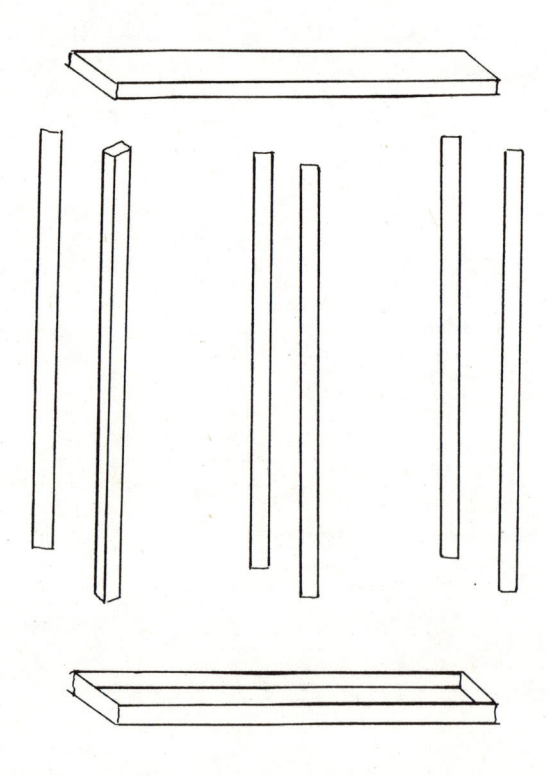

THINGS
TO BUILD
AND HOW

4) attach the hardboard ends, 54″ x 9″, to the frame at each end. Use 1″ brads about every six inches down both sides, top and bottom.

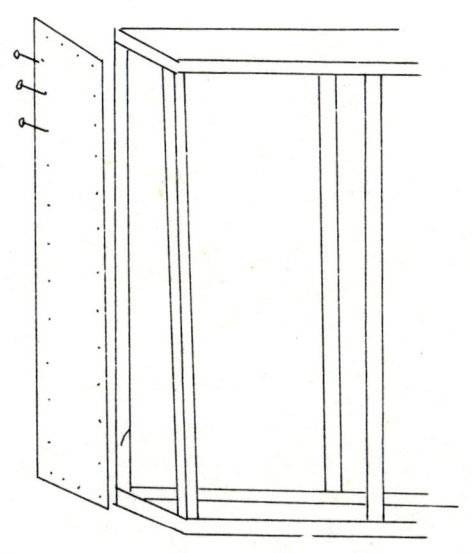

5) Across the base of the supporting frame, nail additional supports 8½″ in length from the back of the frame to the front, at each end and on each side of the center support. At 24½″ from the floor add the first shelf supports, again at each end and on each side

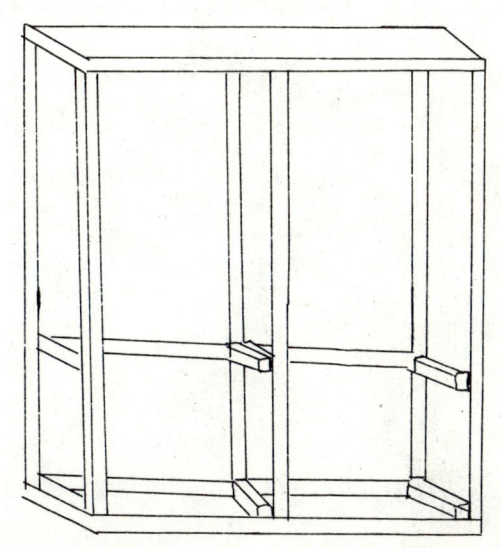

43

of the center support. At this height, also attach supports on the wall between the supports at each end and the center.

6) The lower front sections of the cabinet can now be attached. Nail the 23″ x 23″ ½″ plywood between the main frame 2 x 2 and against ends of the bottom and shelf supports. The shelf supports and the top of these plywood panels should be level with each other.

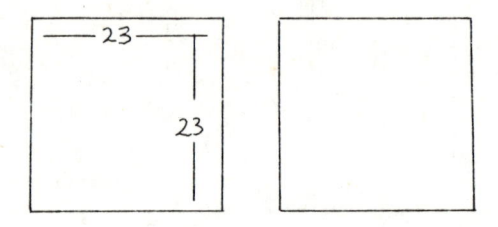

7) The first shelf, 8½″ x 23″, can now be put into position on top of the shelf supports. Although the cabinet is 9″ deep, this first shelf is 8½″ deep to accommodate a fold-up door.

The second shelf, 23″ x 9″, will be 39½″ from floor level. Glue (and nail for additional strength) the shelf supports across the frame as with the lower shelf. You won't need extra support for this shelf.

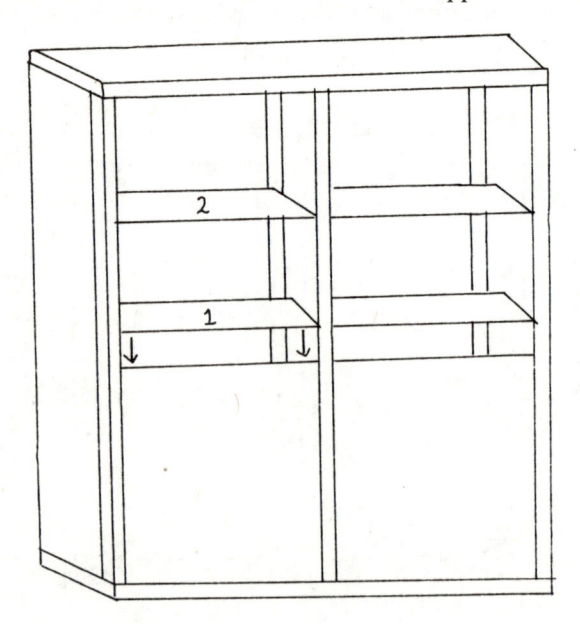

44

8) The first door, 23" x 14", pulls down and is attached with hinges to the top of the ½" plywood front panel. When folded closed, the door rests under the top shelf and rests against the supports of that shelf.

The top section takes two doors, each $11\frac{3}{8}$" x $13\frac{7}{8}$", and they are also attached with hinges.

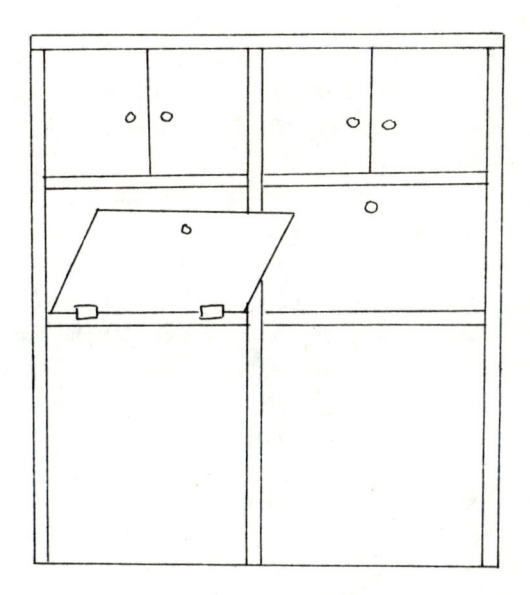

All that remains to be done is sanding, finishing, and the addition of knobs. I used a handle that flushed flat when the door was down. I didn't want a knob sticking in my neck while I was reading. All the other knobs are white porcelain and available in any hardware store.

A Digression

> By the work one knows the workman
> JEAN DE LA FONTAINE, *Fables*

My headboard may not be your headboard, but a cabinet like this, with some adjustments, might just fit into a particular area in your apartment. It would, for example, work well as a desk. The only major difference would be that the two front pieces—the permanent ones measuring 23″ x 23″ in the headboard (and the drop-leaf sections)—would become one piece measuring 23″ x 47½″. The extra 1½″ includes the middle 2 x 2 of the support frame (actually 1½″ wide). That one piece of 2 x 2 would be placed *behind* the front 2 x 2 base (rather than on top of it) and therefore should be 1½″ longer—54″ instead of 53½″ long. The front panel would be nailed against the shelf supports between each end of the frame and into the middle 2 x 2 of the frame. Twenty-three inches aren't high enough to sit at as a desk. A comfortable height is 28″; the front panels can be adjusted accordingly.

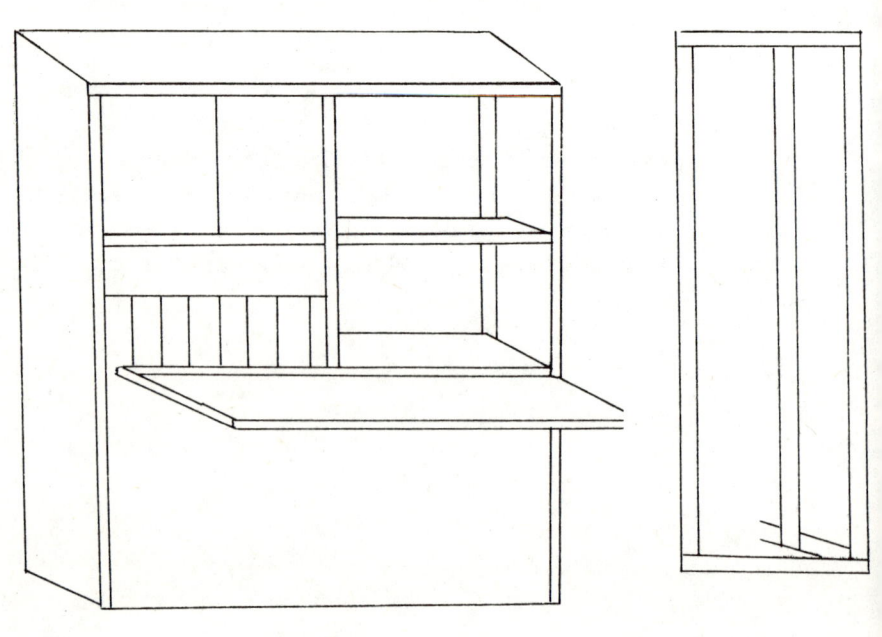

The interior of the desk can be divided into shelves and pigeonholes as you choose; the front panel could be divided into two doors, shelves put in, and what is dead storage space in the headboard would become easily accessible. The drop-leaf of the desk should be attached to the frame with a piano hinge—it'll need that strength if you're working on it—and chains or hinges will hold it steady and support it at writing level.

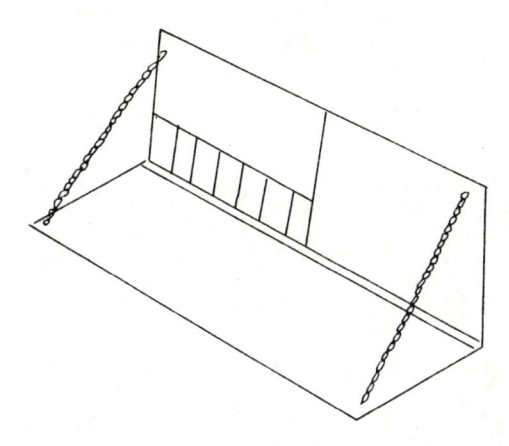

The simple assembly of this cabinet offers lots of options. The desk, for example, does not have to be attached to the wall as the headboard is. The initial step in building the headboard, putting the 52″ shelf on brackets on the wall, needn't be the basis for building the desk. If you wanted to move it from one wall to another, for example, it wouldn't work at all. However, the construction of the permanent headboard and a desk that can be moved around aren't so different that they can't be adapted from the same design.

Furniture is flexible; once you've built one piece, it can be adapted to practically anything else. The design isn't necessarily complicated; the problem is figuring out how to do it. Once you have, there's nothing to stop ideas growing in all directions.

The Wall Unit Again

> Some figures monstrous and misshaped appear,
> Considered singly, or beheld too near,
> Which, but proportioned to their light or place,
> Due distance reconciles to form and grace.
>   POPE, *Essay on Criticism*

The next section of this is very simple: five milk crates $12\frac{1}{2}''$ x $16\frac{1}{2}''$ x $10\frac{1}{2}''$ arranged on top of the shelf, one at each end, and a piece of wood (strips from a cantaloupe crate) placed to create an area between them, and then two more crates on top of that. They'll be quite steady enough without attaching them to each other.

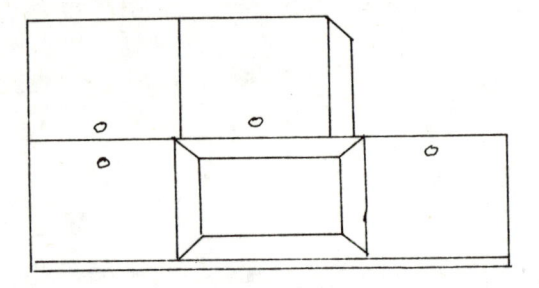

I hinged doors on each of the boxes.

When I first began to run out of storage space and began to think of this monstrous structure, the only firm thing I had in mind was lots of boxes with lots of doors on them, all with white porcelain knobs, all opening in different directions. There's something intriguing about doors looking as if they should be opened—the same fascination as Chinese boxes and intricate miniatures. There's no need to put doors on every box incorporated into any structure. Apart from the delight you might take in lots of cupboard doors waiting to be opened, the only other advantage to doors is that they keep dust out. If you're storing sweaters and other clothes, then they become necessary.

If I'm not always precise about the kinds of boxes I'm using and their sizes, it's because it's not important. You won't always be able to find a milk crate, but you might find a wine crate, and it will work just as well. It depends on the space you're working in and what boxes you can find. Different size boxes can work together (with legs and overhangs as described in the Totem), and you shouldn't be deterred because of difference and variety in boxes—that's where a lot of the fun is.

The next section of the unit was the most complicated, because I had this old chest I didn't want to throw away and nine *different* types of box, mostly of different sizes, too.

Things never work out quite the way you picture them. There's a gap of comprehension somewhere that has to do with space and perspective. It takes experimenting with boxes, in various combinations, before they fit together in the right way. Like jigsaw puzzles, these things do work out, and eventually the boxes and the chest, with the headboard, all worked out into a complete structure.

The chest and the first Chinese box (abalone from Hong Kong) had the same depth of 16", and they went into position alongside each other.

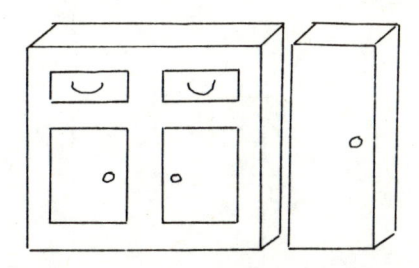

The next box, the closest in size, was a wine box which went on top of the Chinese box:

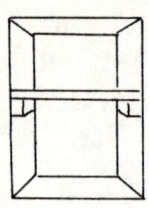

A shelf went into the wine box, and I left the whole thing open. On top of that I stacked two more milk crates:

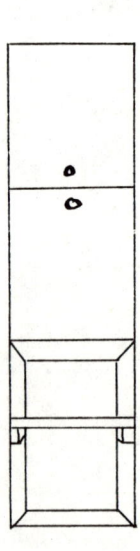

THINGS
TO BUILD
AND HOW

Drawers

*We are not interested in the
possibilities of defeat*
QUEEN VICTORIA TO A. J. BALFOUR

I was pleased with the way it was all going but then, obviously over-confident, I made a disastrous mistake on the next section. I decided to make two drawers to put inside one very large Chinese box. Open any drawer, and its construction (apart from the joints very often used) looks simple enough.

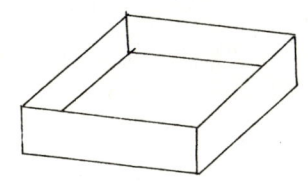

In fact, it looks very much like the base for a small cabinet. In this instance, in order to hang inside the chest, the drawer has to go on some kind of runner. It needs a guide of some kind attached to the inside of the chest and a runner of some kind attached to the drawer. I tried to solve this problem by taking three strips of 1″ wood, two appropriately spaced on each inside side of the box, and one down the center of what was the base/drawer-like thing (which I'd made exactly as if it were a base). It didn't work. It took eight hours of unsuccessful drawers and ruined wood before it finally dawned on me that a drawer is really a box without a top. I found two boxes in my collection that would fit in the major box and work as drawers. The chest of drawers ended up being an absolute fake, but it does work.

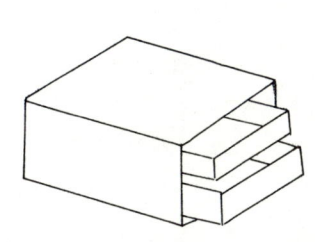

The outside dimensions of the major box are 16″ x 23″, the inside measurements $15\frac{1}{2}$″ x $21\frac{1}{2}$″.

51

The drawers are each of different depths. One box which became a drawer measured 14½″ long x 17″ wide, the other 15″ long x 19½″ wide—both of them quite a bit narrower than the chest/box. But it doesn't matter. To give the top drawer something to rest on, and to slide out from, a shelf went into the chest/box, using a strip of wood on each side to support it. It's ½″ plywood glued down on the support strips of wood.

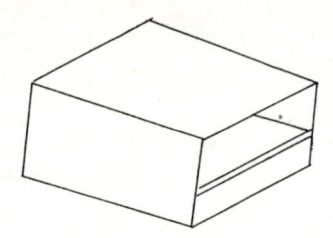

The boxes, which were rapidly becoming drawers, had to look as if they belonged there, at least from the outside. I nailed false fronts on them, which were larger than the actual drawer/boxes but which fit into the dimensions of the chest/box. White porcelain knobs were added.

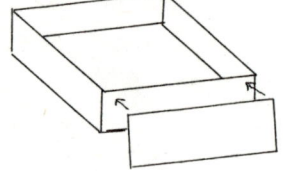

The false fronts are the exact length of the chest/box. The shelf supporting the top box shows between the drawers when they are closed.

So, it doesn't all fit perfectly, and the drawers don't slide evenly or smoothly. But the thing is, they look as if they do.

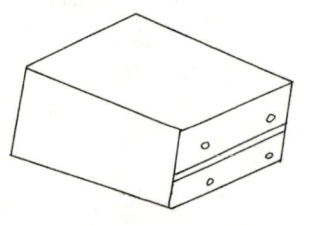

There is another easy way to make a drawer. Once you've accepted the fact that all it is is a box without a top, it can be made easily. Make it just as if it were a base but, because the stress of pulling the drawer out is at the front, nail the front of the drawer *between* the side pieces.

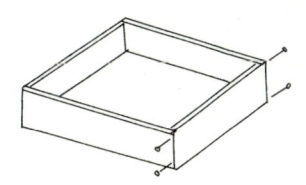

The bottom of the drawer is made either from $\frac{1}{4}''$ plywood or hardboard, which is actually stronger. Tack it into the bottom of the sides of the drawer, putting brads about every $3''$.

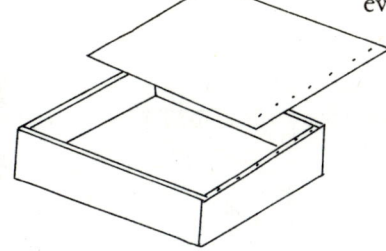

To support the drawer in the case—either a box or cabinet—glue and tack in support strips on each side and at the front. If the drawer is made to *fit* the chest, it won't need the support of a shelf as the mismatched boxes do.

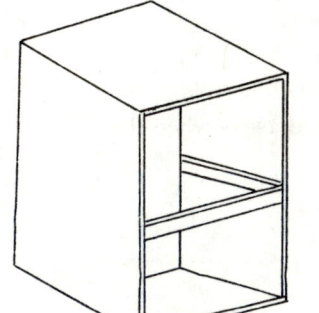

Whenever possible, avoid making drawers. Make a cabinet instead.

Finishing the Wall Unit

> What you see, yet cannot see over,
> is as good as infinite
> THOMAS CARLYLE, *Sartor Resartus*

The rest of it is easy—the box drawers on top of the old chest, and the other two boxes on top of that. What's needed at this point are finishing touches.

None of the boxes are nailed together; they're supported by their own weight and each other. If you used flimsy boxes, such as plum crates, for a structure of any kind, this wouldn't work. They'd have to be joined to each other, and probably to the wall as well.

Because the boxes are all different sizes, cover-ups and adjustments had to be made with odd pieces of wood picked up from the lumberyard or cut down from boxes. Although I didn't level off the top of the unit, preferring the different shaped spaces, it could be done the same way.

The gaps in the left side of the unit (the section supported by the chest) was exposed to anyone walking into the room. It wasn't steady, didn't look finished, and needed some support.

Pieces of wood were cut to size for all the gaps between the two top boxes, which were narrower than the chest (and which supported it all), and the drawers on which they sat. I used a milk crate because that was the strongest wood around. The pieces were glued and wedged between the wall and the backs of the boxes.

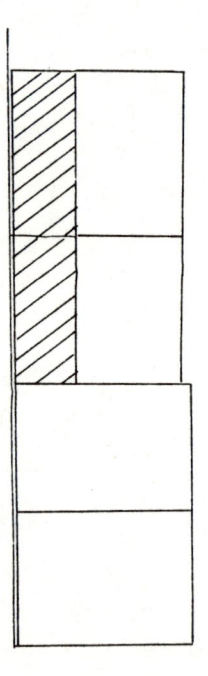

There were also gaps between the boxes from the front view. Again it took a box cut into pieces to fill them. This time, plum crates; strength wasn't needed, just a façade.

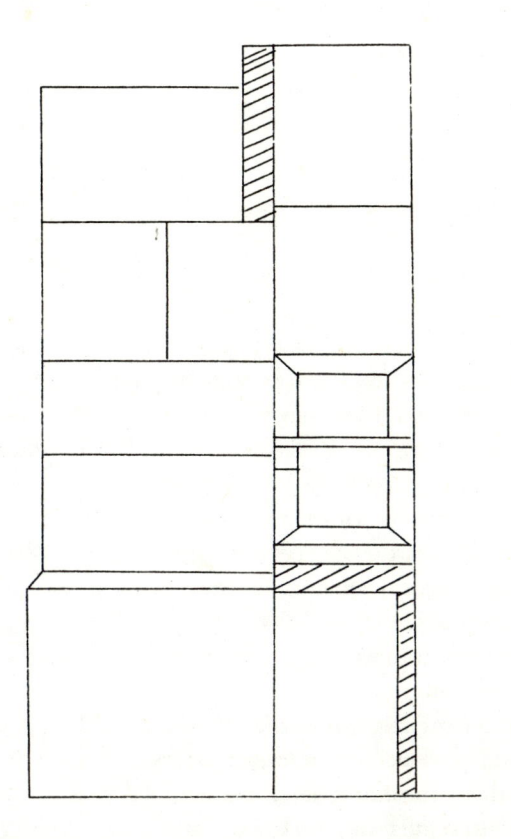

The façades were glued in between the boxes, and the cracks between filled with wood putty. Sanded down and stained, or painted, all the bits and pieces work into the whole unit.

Don't be put off from making anything because the boxes aren't the same size. They can all be adjusted and faked and made to work into the whole. If you're going to wait to find boxes all the same size, you might never make anything. It's true it would be easier, but not as much fun to play around with.

Couches and Other Things to Sit On

> The whitewashed wall, the newly sanded floor,
> The vanish'd clock that click'd behind the door;
> The chest contriv'd a double debt to pay,—
> A bed by night, a chest of drawers by day
> OLIVER GOLDSMITH, *The Deserted Village*

I HAVE A friend who found a heavily upholstered 10' couch on the street. Its condition wasn't bad—a bit worn and missing one leg. He'd just found a new apartment, had no furniture and no money and so, being a thrifty guy (as well as broke), he gathered his friends together to cart the couch away. It involved six people, five flights of narrow stairs, and a living room which measured about 12' x 11'. The couch was not only 10' long but was also about 3' wide, so it quite literally took over the apartment. Unable to part with this free find (and not quite nervy enough to ask his friends to carry it down the staircase again), he lived with it for five months, convincing himself that he loved it. Then he moved, leaving the couch and apartment to a friend. She had a sawing-up party, and the couch went out in pieces.

There is a moral to this tale. It's all very well to have a couch, but it's a big item in both size and expense. Usually it's easier to make something yourself that can be designed so that it fits into the apartment without taking over. In a small apartment you should think particularly of clean, economical lines, of something comfortable but not dominant. Another advantage is that *you* decide on the length—you don't have to stick to standard sizes.

A very simple platform couch can be made with boxes and foam—any boxes with the same height and foam cut to size. Boxes $12\frac{1}{2}''$ in height are a good point to work from. Once these are covered in $4''$ foam, the total height would be $16''$. You want it to be comfortable for lounging, so anything much higher shouldn't be used. This couch was built from eight milk crates ($12\frac{1}{2}''$ high x $10\frac{1}{2}''$

wide); the total length of the couch is 65" and the total width 21".

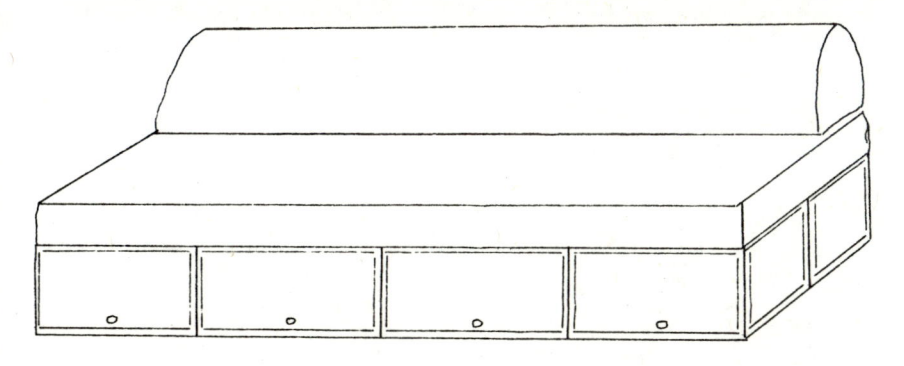

The front row of boxes was placed with the open ends facing into the room; doors were added and storage space created. Foam bolsters can be cut to length and lean directly against the wall. At night, these can be taken off the couch to make a bed—for a short guest. If the couch is made one milk crate length longer and one deeper, it becomes a bed of decent size.

To add arms to the couch, use $\frac{3}{4}"$ plywood panels and attach one to the boxes at each end. The height of the seat is $16\frac{1}{2}"$ from the floor (that's $12\frac{1}{2}"$ of milk crate plus $4"$ of foam). Add $6"$ for the arms, and the total height comes to $22\frac{1}{2}"$. The plywood panels for this couch were cut to $21 \times 22\frac{1}{2}"$.

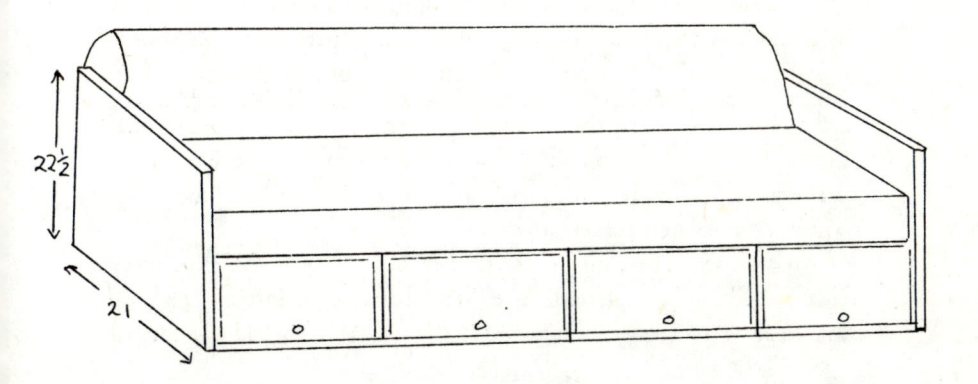

Another lounging place, free of the wall, can be built in a similar way. This can be effective and decorative if you use a combination of boxes—perhaps milk and orange crates:

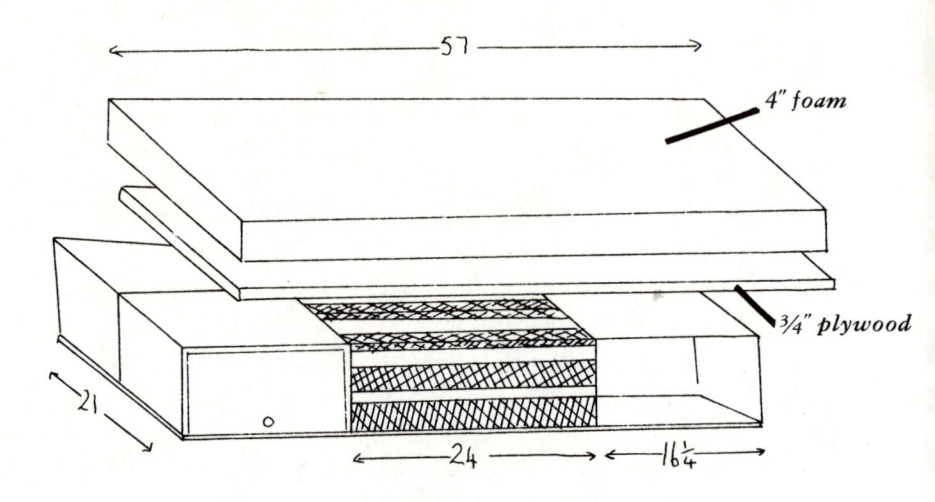

It's not necessary to use the $\frac{3}{4}''$ plywood, but it will look more solid if you do. Also, boxes with slats, such as orange crates, can cause the foam to sink in between them and then you get that lumpy feeling when you sit down. If you decide to use the plywood platform, it should be cut to the same size as the outside dimensions of the boxes when placed together.

An advantage to using a mixture of box types is the effect they create. I like to use slatted boxes with solid ones, just to break up that feeling of heavy, solid wood. If you want to add a door, or doors, to the milk crates, it works well. You might prefer, though, to leave the whole thing open.

Although you might feel the couch eats up too much space, these platforms can be attractive and break up a room. Throw some cushions over the covered foam and it's comfortable for lounging or sleeping. It's a great way to make a bed in a studio apartment. Rather than using sheets and blankets that have to be made up all the time, it's easier to use a comforter (some of them come in sleeping bag form) to wrap around you. It's also easier to store underneath the platform in one of those boxes with a door on it. Another box will take the pillows.

While waxing strong on orange crate slats, I should mention that they work well with this platform when you put a small lamp or colored bulb inside them. They create a marvellous shadowy glow in a dark room when all the other lights are off.

Chairs

> Here will we sit, and let the
> sounds of music
> creep in our ears
> SHAKESPEARE, *Merchant of Venice*

You're building everything yourself and don't want to spend much money, but this is no time to keep away from department stores. They're stocked with all kinds of furniture which you won't want to buy but which will spark off your own design ideas. The problem becomes one of adapting the furniture in stores to cheaper versions you can build yourself without spending much money. This usually means plywood.

The basic designs of furniture are very simple, whatever the object might be. You have to be able to see through the elaboration of decoration, style, fabrics, and materials. A chair is not as impossible to make as it may seem. Once you can see its form, the problem is only one of angles. After all, they're nearly all squared into a box form, whether it's with four legs or an upholstered, enclosed base; whether it's a wicker chair, or a sofa, with arms or without. They all have an area to sit in, a support of legs or solid base, and a back to lean on. Once you've figured out the pieces it's only a matter of putting them together strongly so that the whole thing doesn't collapse the first time you sit on it.

Once you begin to see the way furniture is put together, to reduce it to its basic form, you can begin to adapt it to your own needs, using different, cheaper materials, putting them together differently perhaps, but maintaining the basic form which is often what attracted you to a particular piece of furniture in the first place. And there's no reason why you can't copy the things you see around you. And you'll end up not copying exactly because your apartment, your needs, will finally dictate what you do, how you make it.

This chair began just that way. There's nothing complicated about it, so I wasn't distracted into thinking I couldn't in some way reproduce it. I found a chair, similar to this, at a store known for its modern furniture. It caught my eye. I went back with a tape measure the next day. I had no idea what kind of angles were used in placing the back and arms comfortably, no idea how high the average chair should be, the width of the seat, or even how I might be able to make a chair something like it. It's a very simple, solid wooden frame with foam rubber cushions cut to size and covered with fabric. In the store it was made from laminated birchwood and finely finished. As it is now, in my apartment, it's made from $\frac{3}{4}''$ plywood.

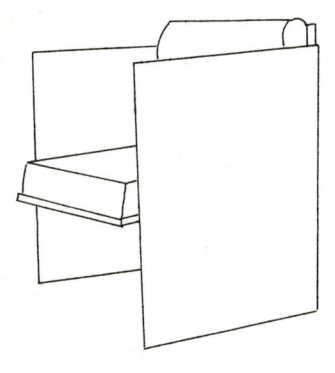

There was no problem taking measurements: As far as the store knew, I was measuring for space in my apartment. Actually, I was self-conscious about my measuring activities, and it took three days to get them down properly. Finally, all measurements in hand, I went off to the lumberyard and ordered the plywood cut to size.

Plywood comes in standard 4' x 8' sheets; two chairs can be cut from that. It's usually cheaper to buy the whole sheet rather than sections of it, so before going to buy the wood, work out the dimensions of what you'll need—it might save you some money. For this chair, you will need to use $\frac{3}{4}''$ plywood, graded smooth on both sides, (see chapter on lumber). Two 22" x 26" pieces for the sides, one 20" x 18" piece for the back, and a seat 20" x 22". You will also need support strips, one 19" in length and the other 12". Use scraps from the sheet of plywood for the supports. Make sure you tell the lumberman you want them. If you want only one chair, buy half a sheet of plywood (4' x 4'); you'll still have scraps for supports.

THE BOX
BOOK

Laid out on a 4' x 8' sheet of plywood, the pieces of the chair will look like this:

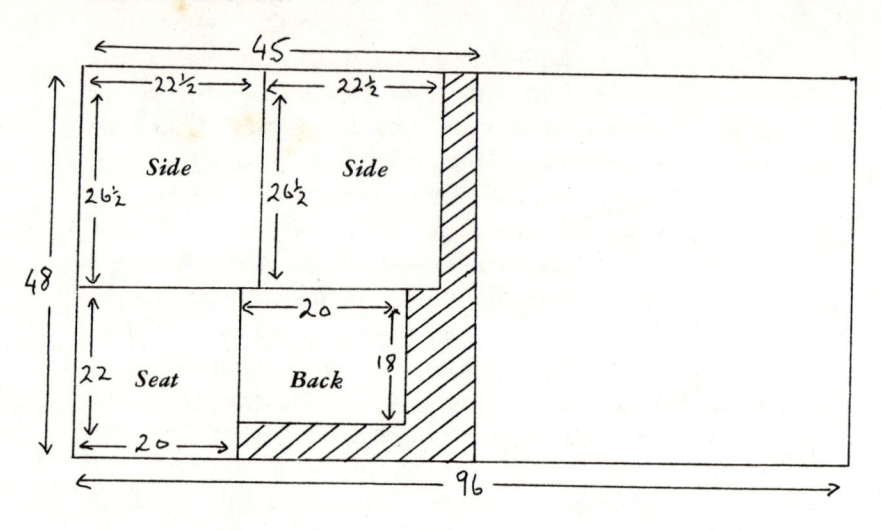

(diagram: plywood layout 48 × 96, showing two Sides 22½ × 26½, Seat 20 × 22, Back 20 × 18)

You will also need eighteen 1¼" wooden finishing screws and some epoxy glue.

side of chair

The 19" and 12" support strips used on the chairs are 1½" high and 1" thick. It doesn't matter if the supports you use are only 1" or 2" high; but do adjust the first measurements. A total of 12" from the floor (plus foam cushion) is a comfortable sitting height

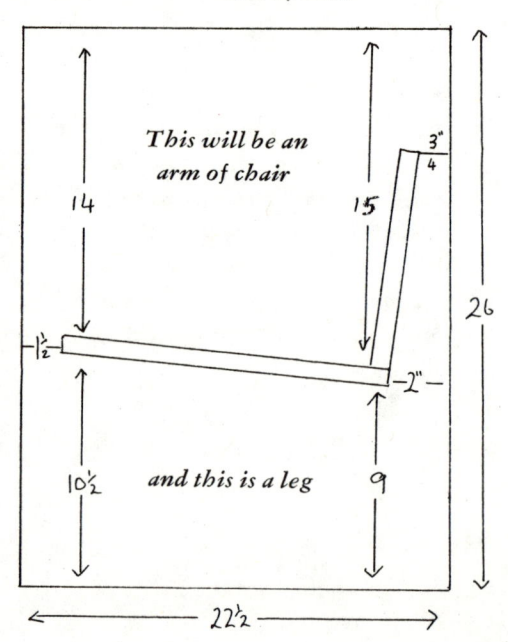

(diagram: side of chair, 22½ × 26, showing arm of chair and leg with measurements 14, 15, 3/4, 1½, 2, 10½, 9)

62

1) The seat and back of the chair will rest on, and be attached to, the support strips of wood. The seat strip should be 19″ long and the back strip 12″ long.

2) Place the sides of the chair on the floor, with the side you choose as the outside of the chair down. Measure from the bottom $10\frac{1}{2}''$ at the front and 9″ at the back. Draw a pencil line between the two points. The support strip will rest along this line, which gives the angle at which the seat will be placed. The support will be 2″ in from the side at the back of the chair.

3) The back support should rest on the end of the seat support. At the top it will be $\frac{3}{4}''$ in from the side and 2″ in at the bottom. Pencil in a line between these two points.

4) Glue along the lines drawn on the side of the chair, and on the edges of the supports. Place them in position and leave them to dry.

5) When the supports are firm, turn the chair sides over. To give proper support, screws will go in from the outside. You should *measure* on this side of the chair, too. (Remember which is front and

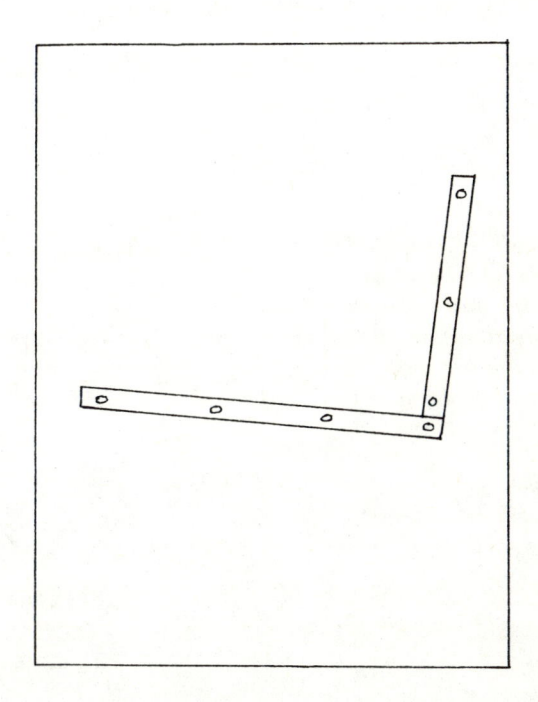

back of the chair for proper heights.) It's too easy, when putting in the screws, to miss the supports by a fraction of an inch and ruin the whole thing.

Outside of chair with outline of supports glued on the inside. Use four $1\frac{1}{2}''$ wood screws from the outside to hold the seat support and three $1\frac{1}{2}''$ wood screws for the back support. Use finishing screws and make sure the head is screwed just slightly beneath the surface of the wood. They will be covered by wood cement before finishing. The supports are now firm for the seat and back pieces of the chair.

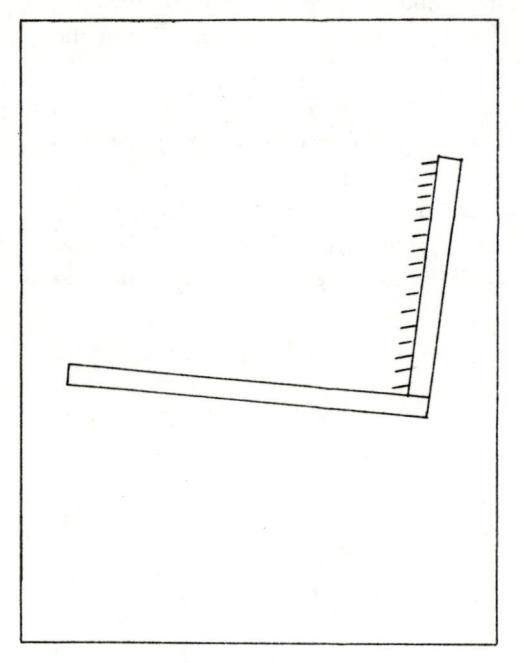

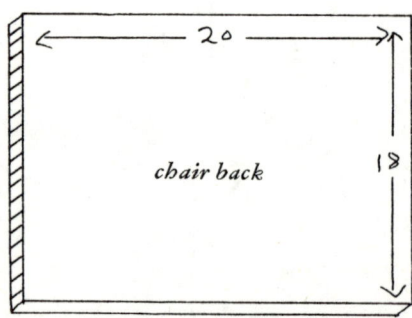

It's easier if you work with the first side of the chair on the floor. Glue the two areas shaded in the sketch; this is the first step in attaching the back rest to the side of the chair. Put them together and hold them in place until the back and side are firmly fixed to each other. (That's why it's easier to have the chair side on the floor.) When it's dry, you can place the screws through the back of the chair into its support.

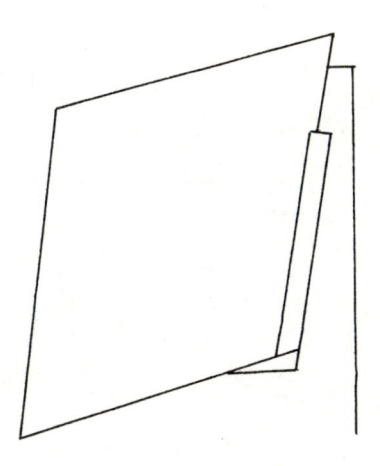

The seat can now be glued in position. Glue the edges of the support, the bottom of the chair back, and one side edge of the seat, which already has the supports attached. Glue all the edges and place it all together.

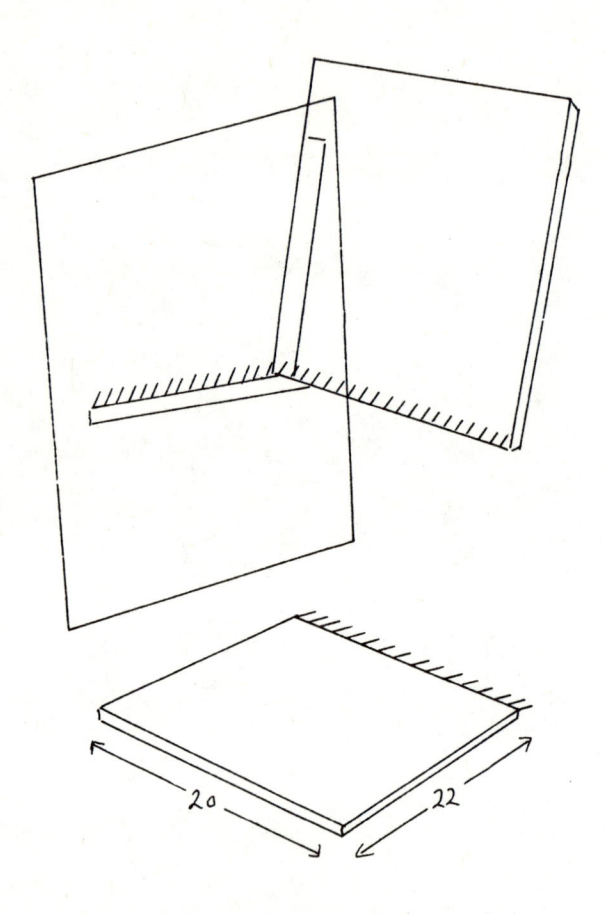

Do not move the chair until it is absolutely dry, firm, and unmovable at all joints. Now you can place it upright and put wood screws through the seat and back into the supports.

THINGS
TO BUILD
AND HOW

The same basic design used in the chair can be adapted for what is called, in department stores and advertisements, a "love seat"; it's really a two-seater couch, and a combination of two chair widths would give you one. A more comfortable, roomier couch can be made if you allow three chair widths.

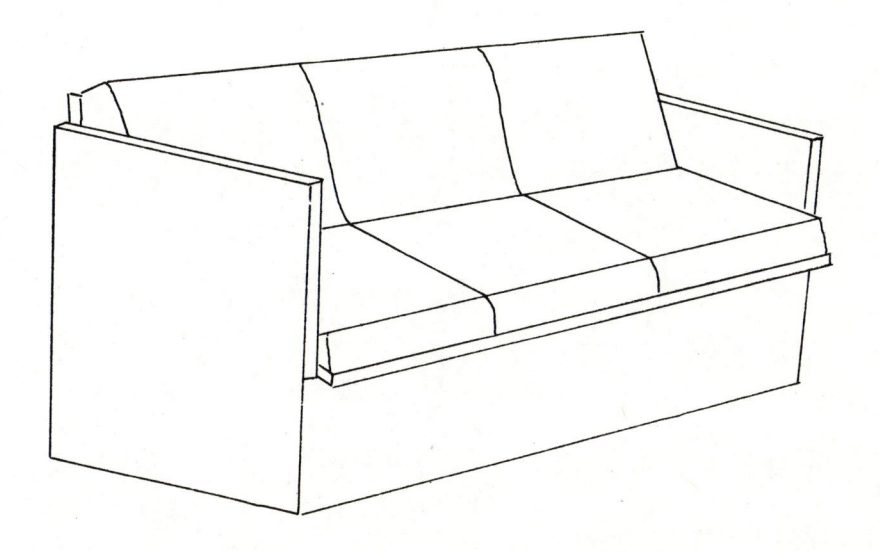

The seat and back of the chair are each 20″ wide; for couch width or length, triple it to 60″. The depths of the seat and height of back remain at 18″ and 22″ respectively. Procedure for making the couch is exactly that of making the chair. It will need some additional support however. This can be done by adding a central leg support in the middle of the seating section. Ask the lumberyard to cut a piece of $\frac{3}{4}$″ plywood to the following dimensions:

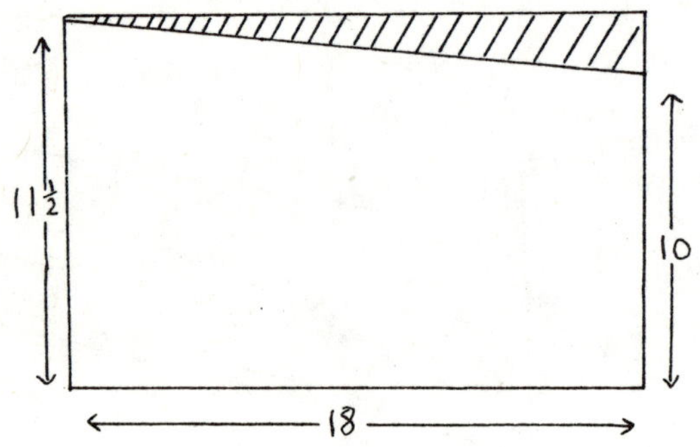

The side heights of 11½″ and 10″ allow for height from the floor to the underside of the seating section, plus the 1″ height of the seat support strips. The depth of the couch is 22″, but the central leg support need only be 18″ and can be placed 2″ in from the front and back of the couch.

THINGS
TO BUILD
AND HOW

To finish the whole thing off really effectively, put a front panel under the seating section, against the legs of the couch, enclosing it all in a box-like frame.

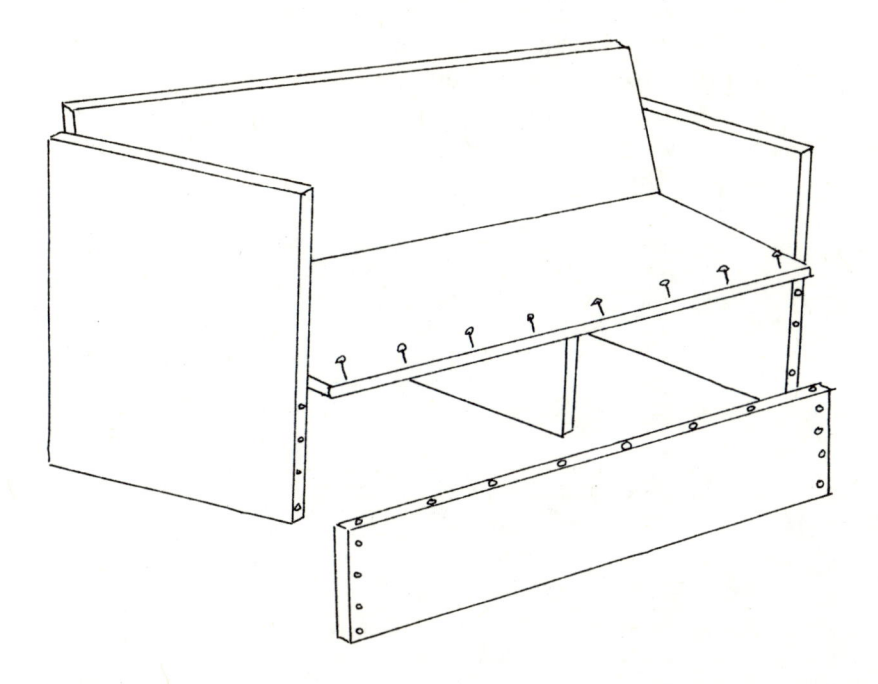

Inset the panel under the seat, against the leg sections of each side, and screw it together. Glue all edges first for additional support. It is possible to use $\frac{1}{4}''$ plywood for this. It would create a façade, but it wouldn't have real strength. Better are $\frac{1}{2}''$ or $\frac{3}{4}''$ plywood. They're thick enough to use an additional screw through the top of the seat into the edge of the plywood. If you want the couch "floating" in the room, you might add a back panel of plywood in similar fashion.

Don't be restricted by any of these dimensions, especially lengths. The length of the couch can be made to fit wherever you want. The basic design, however, remains the same. The cushions can be cut into three sections, as in the sketch, or more, or even used in one length. It's all flexible.

Plywood is heavy, and this isn't a lightweight couch that can be easily shifted around. But no couch is, and this is somewhat more flexible than the standard upholstered ones. When moving to a new apartment, and particularly if you're carrying it yourself, the couch can, with a little care, be easily taken apart, stacked, and reassembled in the new place.

THINGS
TO BUILD
AND HOW

Seat Covers and How to Make Them

>Silently as a dream the fabric rose,
>No sound of hammer or of saw was there
>WILLIAM COWPER, *The Task*

When I was seven years old, a teacher pointed out that I was the worst seamstress the school had ever seen. Immediately, my desire to please my sewing teacher disappeared, and to this day I still can't sew well and have little desire to. However, I've been forced into a semblance of sewing because of all those foam rubber cushions that needed covering. Friends with sewing machines will often make covers for you, but that only goes so far. You're embarrassed to ask again; they're busy, or they don't have sewing machines, and so forth.

Actually, the pattern for a cover isn't very complicated. The painful part is sewing the pieces together. Not only do I find it difficult to give the stitches some degree of evenness, but they must be sewn so that the whole thing ends up being durable. And the needle is painful to fumbling fingers. At least it's worth the try and certainly cheaper than having the covers made professionally.

There are, of course, all kinds of fabrics, and you'll want a sturdy, inexpensive one. Corduroy, burlap, canvas, duck (a kind of canvas, but softer), denim, and felt have interesting textures and can be handled with a minimum of stitching. To avoid too much fraying of the fabric, it's worth investing in a pair of pinking shears, which have serrated edges and somehow cut fabrics so that they don't fray. For sewing these fabrics, you'll need a large needle and unbreakable nylon thread.

The seat cushions for the chair on page 61 are 22″ x 20″ x 4″, and you will need approximately 1 yard of fabric for each cover. Fabrics come in standard widths of 36″, 42″, and 45″; there are others but these are the main ones. What length you'll need depends on the width of the material you're using. Cut the pattern out of newspaper before you go to buy the fabric, then match it all up at the store.

You'll need two pieces of material 21″ x 23″ for the top and bottom of the cover. (The extra 1″ on each side allows for ½″ seams all the way round.) You will also need four strips of material 5″ wide and 21″ long. Sew them between the top and bottom of the cover with ½″ hems to give the 4″ height you need for the foam rubber cushions which will go inside the cover. Attach the fourth side separately, so that fasteners can be placed there. Some kind of fastening is essential so that the covers can be taken off for cleaning. Work on the cushion inside-out, so that all the stitching won't show when it's on the cushion.

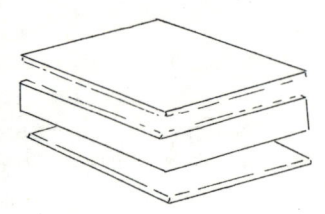

The 5″ strip of material is sewn between and to the top and bottom pieces. The seams will be ½″ on the three sides.

Unless you can already sew, forget thoughts of a zipper to close the opening at the back of the cover. They're not easy to put in, and if they're not put in right, they won't work. Either don't bother with any kind of fastener or use a wonderful thing called Velcro. This fastener is bought by the inch, is ½″ wide, and comes in two strips which are sewn to each edge of the materials to be fastened. Press the strips together, and the edges are closed. They can be separated just as easily.

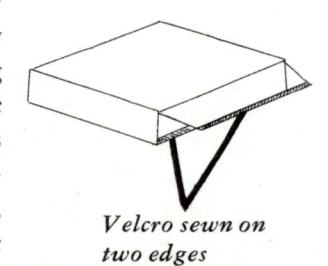

Velcro sewn on two edges

THINGS
TO BUILD
AND HOW

This cover can be made to fit any size cushion, but when it comes to really large covers—on a couch for example—it can become very tedious. There is a way to get round all of that sewing. If you want to cover the seat of a couch and you're using a piece of foam 30" long x 24" wide x 4" high, buy a piece of fabric which you can literally wrap around the foam. It should be a good 6" longer and wider than the dimensions of the couch. The idea is to lace the edges of the fabric together.

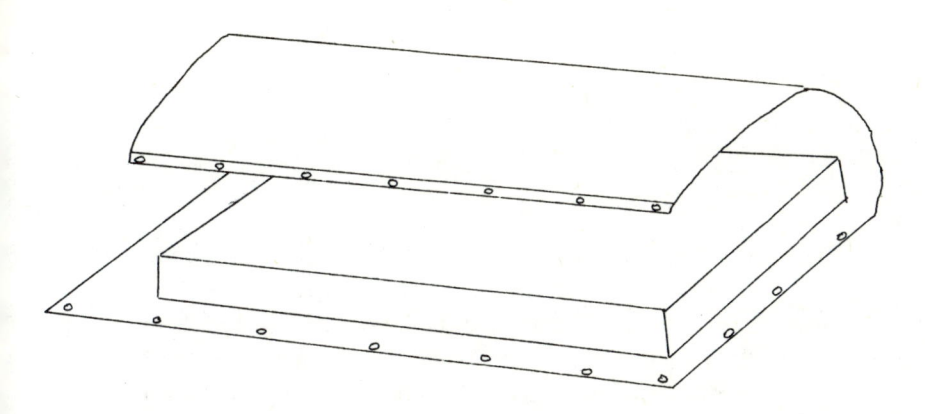

Make a hem on the edges of the fabric by folding it back ½". You'll need a hole-punch and some metal eyelets to press into the holes. The holes will go through the hem (two thicknesses) and be held in place by the metal eyelets which you punch into the fabric. The hole-punch and eyelets can be bought at craft stores and some Five-and-Tens. Line the eyelets up evenly on both edges of the fabric and then lace them together with strips of leather, thick wool (the kind that's sold to wrap packages), or even rope. Decide on this before you buy the eyelets; rope, for example, will need large holes, and you'll need big eyelets.

Bookshelves

> Where are your books—that light bequeathed
> To beings else forlorn and blind!
> WILLIAM WORDSWORTH, *Expostulation and Reply*

The easiest thing in the world is to stack up a bunch of boxes and call them bookshelves. If you use larger boxes, such as orange or milk crates, they won't need any joining together or bracketing to the wall. Wine crates, or other smaller or narrower boxes, will. But it's easy enough to put a screw between every box and attach the top boxes to the wall with brackets. If you're doing a whole wall this way it can look a bit too heavy for the room, but if you paint them in white enamel or other light colors, they can work out well. Smaller wall areas are particularly good places to stack boxes for bookcases or other storage.

Building a bookcase from planks of wood is not very difficult either, though it takes a little more time, costs more, and you have to be sure to get the measurements right. As furniture building goes, bookshelves are the easiest. They're sometimes awkward if they're tall and you're working in a small apartment, but still easy.

I have three units on one wall covering an area 8'6" high x 7'6" wide; they're made from knotty pine and worked out to cost about $60—the most expensive furniture in the whole place, but still a quarter of what they would have cost at a store.

THINGS
TO BUILD
AND HOW

It's best to build large areas of bookcases in sections. The width of any single section shouldn't be more than 4′ and preferably 3′. Wood "breathes" (which means warps), and the weight of too many books on any one shelf can make it sag if it's too long. Also, using 3′ or 4′ widths makes it easier to handle when building and easier to move when you're moving to a new apartment. For this reason, and one of extra strength, mine are also backed with $\frac{1}{4}''$ plywood.

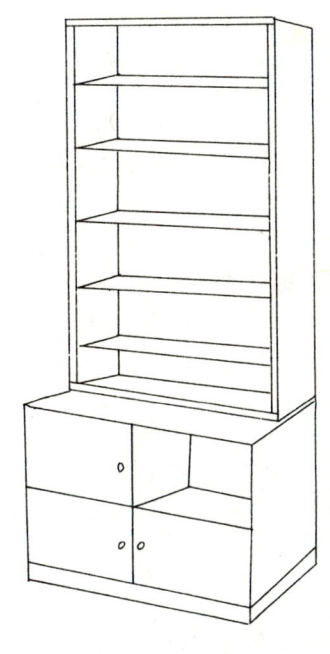

Knotty pine planking for shelves comes in standard widths of 9″ (8⅝) and 12″ (11¾). Unless you want to include shelves for records or unusually large books—perhaps encyclopedias or art books—9″ is a good depth and will take most books. A combination of 12″ and 9″ shelves can be worked out. A couple of wider shelves at the bottom, on which you can put doors for cabinets, with 9″ bookcases placed on top works well.

For one 3′ wide x 8′6″ high bookcase, for example, you'll need the following materials: The height, of course, depends on the height of your own ceiling. It makes things easy if the height of the bookcase is 6″ lower than the ceiling.

1) Two pieces of knotty pine 9″ x 8′6″
2) One piece of 1 x 3, 3′ long
3) Ten pieces of knotty pine 9″ x 3′
4) 37½″ x 84½″ piece of ¼″ plywood for backing
5) Two metal braces
6) About fifty 3″ nails and fifty 1″ brads

Allow about 10″ space between each shelf. Don't forget to allow approximately 1″ for the space occupied by every shelf. The

75

shelves don't have to be spaced evenly; one way to decide on shelf heights is to measure your books and build shelves which allow for different sizes.

1) Put the two pieces of 9" x 8'6" knotty pine, which will be the sides of the bookcase, side-by-side on the floor. Measure and mark where the base, each shelf, and the top of the bookcase will be nailed. With the two planks aligned, it's easy to measure and mark them both at the same time, making sure that when they're nailed the shelves will be straight.

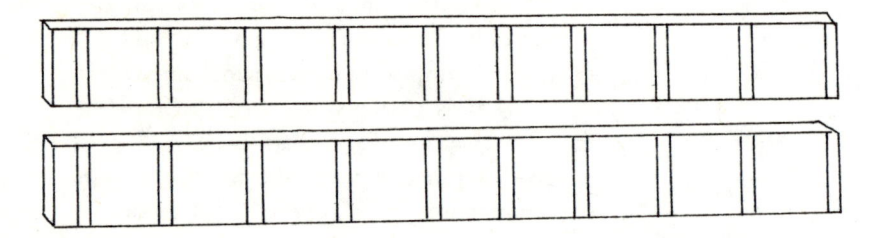

2) The 1 x 3 base can now be fixed in place. It should be recessed from the front of the bookcase about $\frac{1}{2}$"—that is, with the bookcase face down to the floor, $\frac{1}{2}$" off the floor. Use a book which is about $\frac{1}{2}$" thick under each end of the 1 x 3 to hold it in position while you're nailing it in.

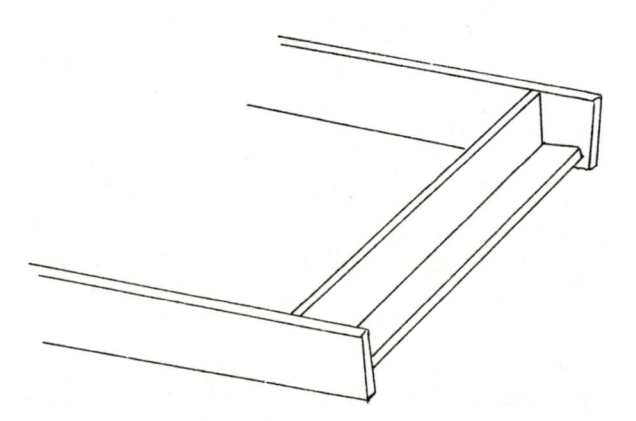

3) The other shelves (the 9" x 3' pieces of knotty pine) can now be nailed into position, and the bookcase is practically finished.

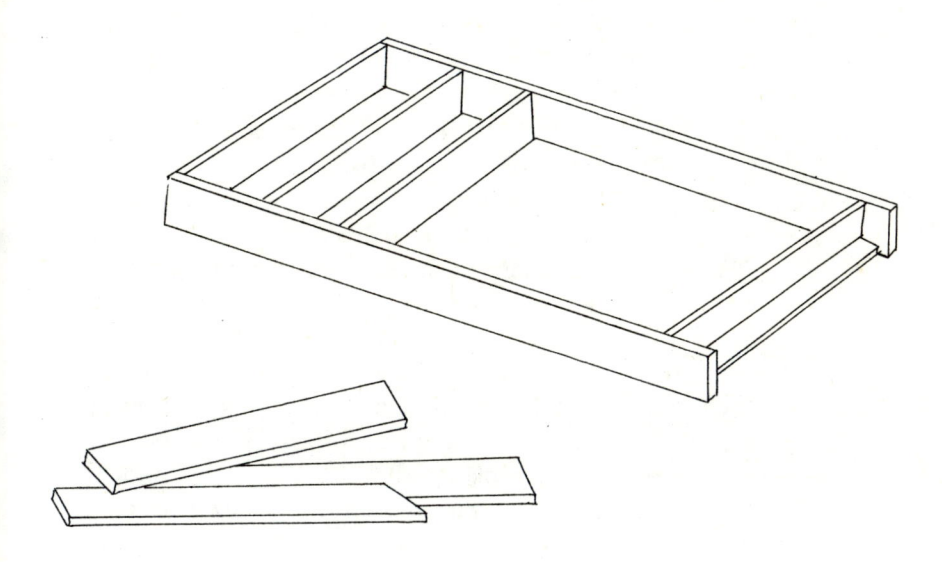

4) If you want to add the ¼" plywood backing, leave the bookcase lying on the floor and tack the backing into position with 1" brads all the way around.

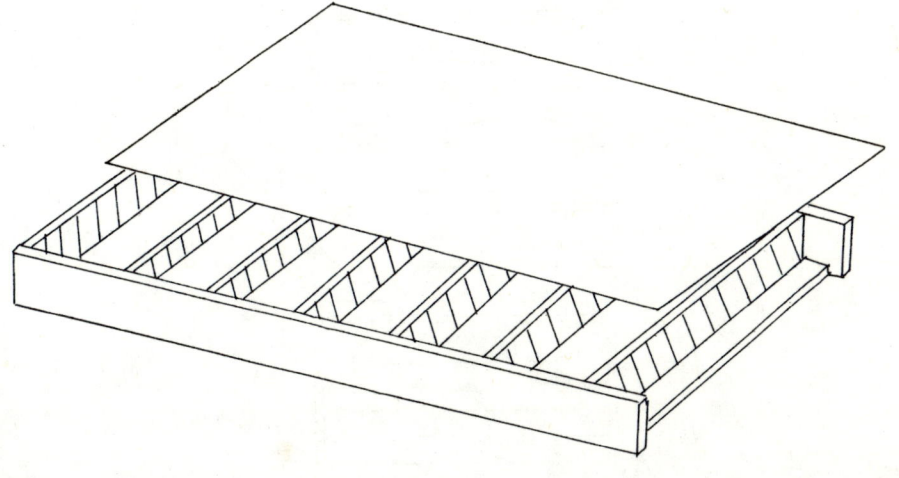

When ordering the backing, remember that it should take into account the *outside* dimensions of the bookcase—36″ wide *plus* the thickness of the side planks, which are ¾″ each, making a total of 37½″ wide for the whole unit. The same accommodation should be made for the height, too. However, it shouldn't go to the floor, but to the bottom shelf.

If you use the ¼″ plywood backing, be careful that you're not covering a bottom shelf which falls in front of any electrical outlets. It's hard to cut the right piece out of the backing to give access to the outlet. Instead, take the backing down to the second shelf and leave the bottom one free of any backing at all.

5) To attach the bookcase to the wall use two small braces.

The bookcase can be made with adjustable rather than permanent shelves. Metal runners with evenly spaced holes and metal shelf supports can be bought by the foot at any hardware store. They should be attached to the sides of the bookcase before nailing the top, first shelf, and base between them. The length of the shelves, for this same 3′ bookcase, should be cut to 35½″ rather than 36″ long. The metal runners take up the difference in the length of shelves. The top of the bookcase, the first shelf, and the 1 x 3 base, however, should be 36" long, as they are part of the frame and attached to the sides of the bookcase with nails. The whole unit will not be as sturdy as the bookcase with permanent shelves, even with the $\frac{1}{4}"$ plywood backing. You should put corner braces into each corner of the bookcase for additional strength. Once the bookcase is up, attached to the wall, with the books on the shelves, it will be quite firm enough.

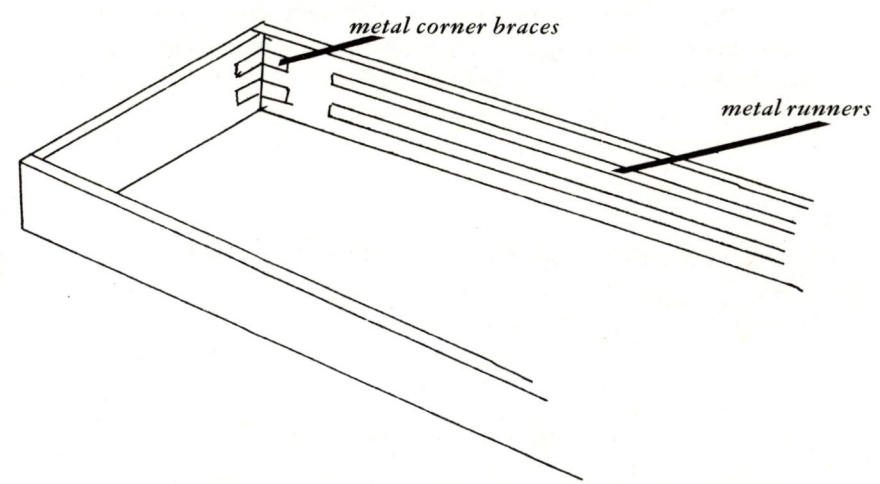

metal corner braces

metal runners

If you do make adjustable shelves, it's worth investing in a brace and bit. Not only is it a tool for drilling holes, but it will drive the screws into the wood and relieve you of the tedium and calluses which result from putting the screws in with a regular old screwdriver. My 8'6" x 7'6" three-sectioned bookcases took 144 screws, all done the slow, hard way. It was time-consuming and painful.

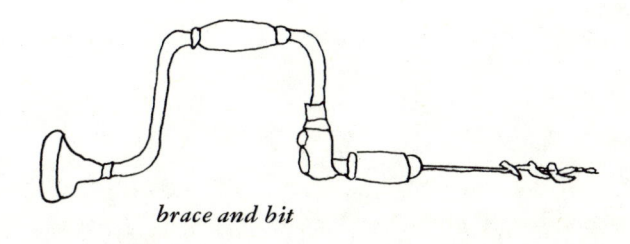

brace and bit

You might think, from reading this, that all bookshelves go against walls. They don't, of course. They're great room dividers, but if you use them for that, they should have permanent shelves and the plywood backing. I've got a very narrow bookcase separating the kitchen from the living room. Because it is so narrow (only 7″), it needed some support; at each end it's attached to the floor by small brackets, and at one end only (the other one is to walk around) it's attached to the wall. If you're making wider, and smaller, bookcases you won't need to support them in this way, although it's always a good idea to attach the bookcase at least to the floor.

Tables

> You may scold a carpenter who has made you a
> bad table, though you cannot make a table.
> It is not your trade to make tables.
> Dr. Johnson, *Boswell's Life of Johnson*

Once you've got the bookcase, it can be adapted for cupboards (by attaching doors to some of the shelves) and tables. Although tables take up space, they don't have to be folding, or narrow, or placed against a wall out of the way. Depending on the shape of your apartment, the space and what else you have, a table can be placed in the middle of a room, drop from a bookcase, or be placed behind a couch.

My apartment has enough room for one decent-sized table. It's both a coffee and dining table. The bookcases are built in three sections on one wall; the middle section was designed with the idea of making the coffee table double as a dining table by raising its height.

The table top is a piece of $\frac{3}{4}''$ plywood measuring $35\frac{1}{2}'' \times 48''$. It has flat molding around the edges, and the whole thing is carefully finished and stained. At coffee table height, it rests on two milk crates, stands $13\frac{1}{4}''$ high, and is level with the second shelf of the bookcase.

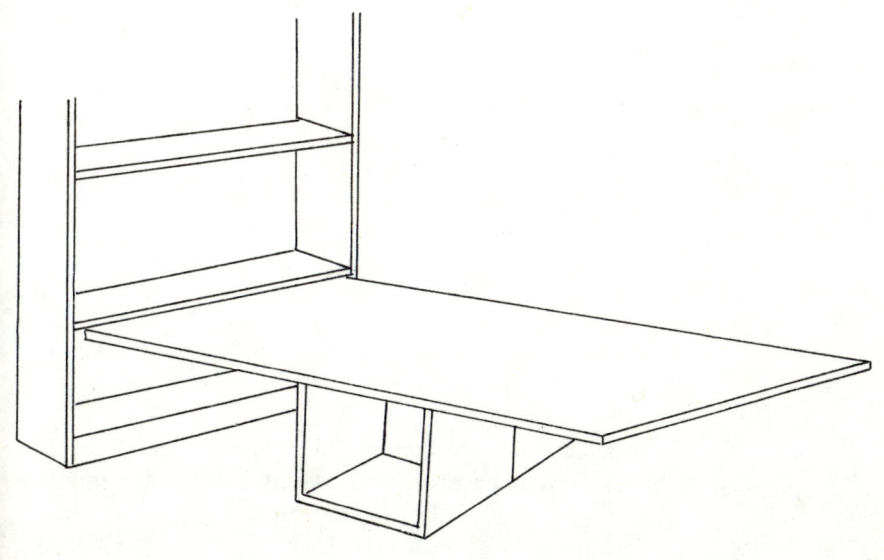

The standard height of a dining table is 29″, which is not, I've discovered, the most comfortable height to eat from—at least not on my chairs. I find 28″ or even 27″ much more comfortable.

The third shelf of the bookcase is 29″ from floor level. An inch below that, I attached two strips of 1 x 1 wood to each side of the bookcase with glue and nails.

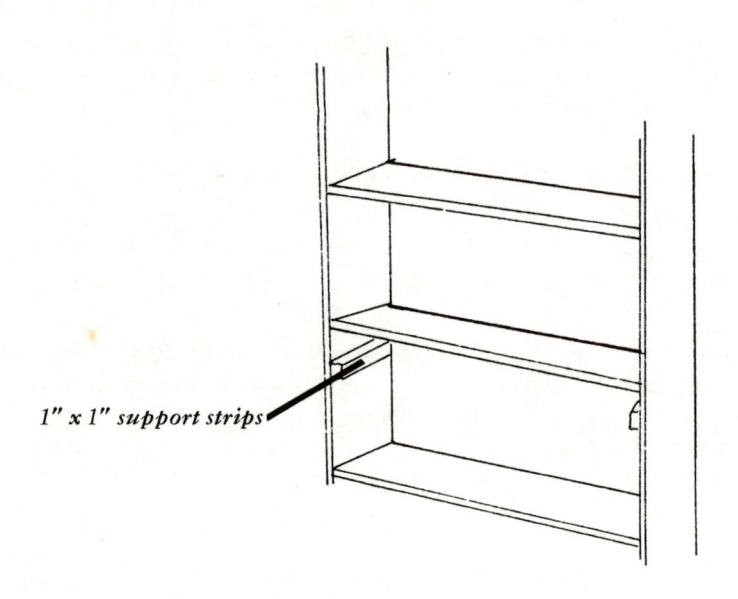

1″ x 1″ support strips

The coffee table became a dining table when a ¾″ piece of plywood 18″ x 27″ was attached to the underside of the table top with a piano hinge so that it became the folding leg. It's centered from each side of the table and 9″ in from the free end. (The other meets the bookcase.) The leg is wide enough so that when it's folded under the coffee table, resting on the milk crate base, it doesn't wobble.

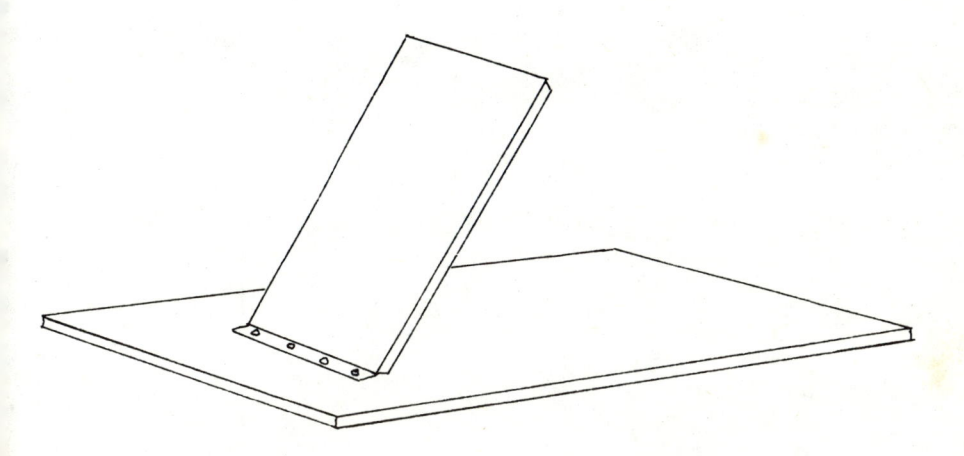

By lifting the coffee table, dropping the leg, sliding the other end of the table underneath the third shelf, and resting it on the supports at each side, it becomes a dining table which, in a pinch, seats five. The milk crates that supported it as a coffee table are either left underneath (so you can put your feet on them) or put to one side until you're ready to lower the table to coffee table height again.

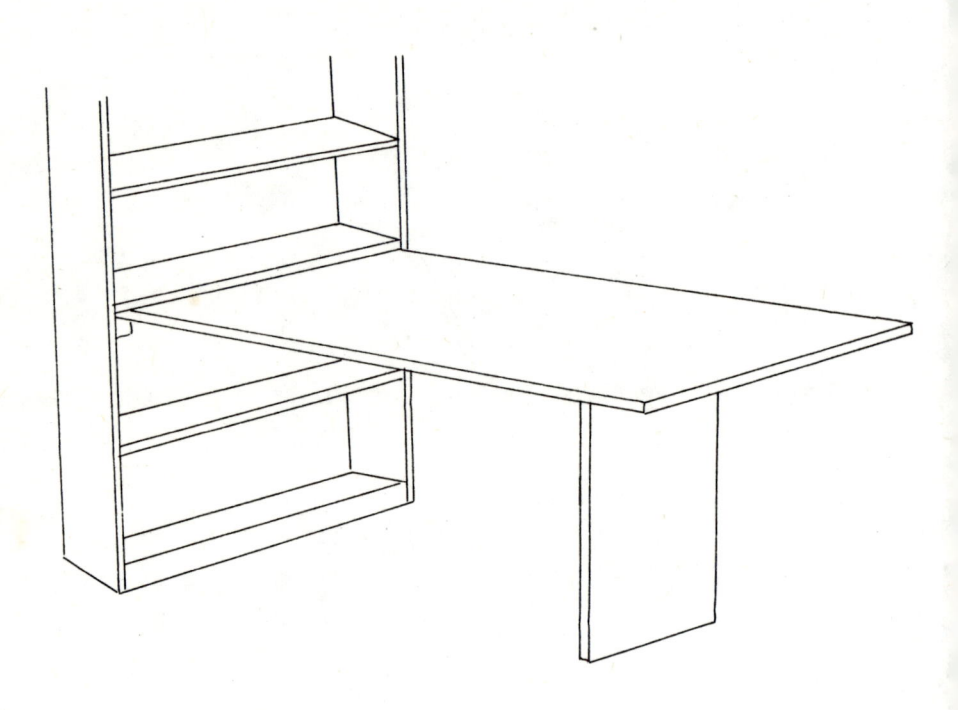

You might not want to take up this kind of space with a coffee or dining table, but the same piece of plywood can be used, with the same plywood folding leg, to build a table that folds directly into the bookcase.

THINGS
TO BUILD
AND HOW

Instead of one end of the table resting underneath the third shelf, it is hinged directly to a permanent shelf of the bookcase, at, of course, the appropriate height, say 27″ or 28″. The table folds into the bookcase rather than being lifted up.

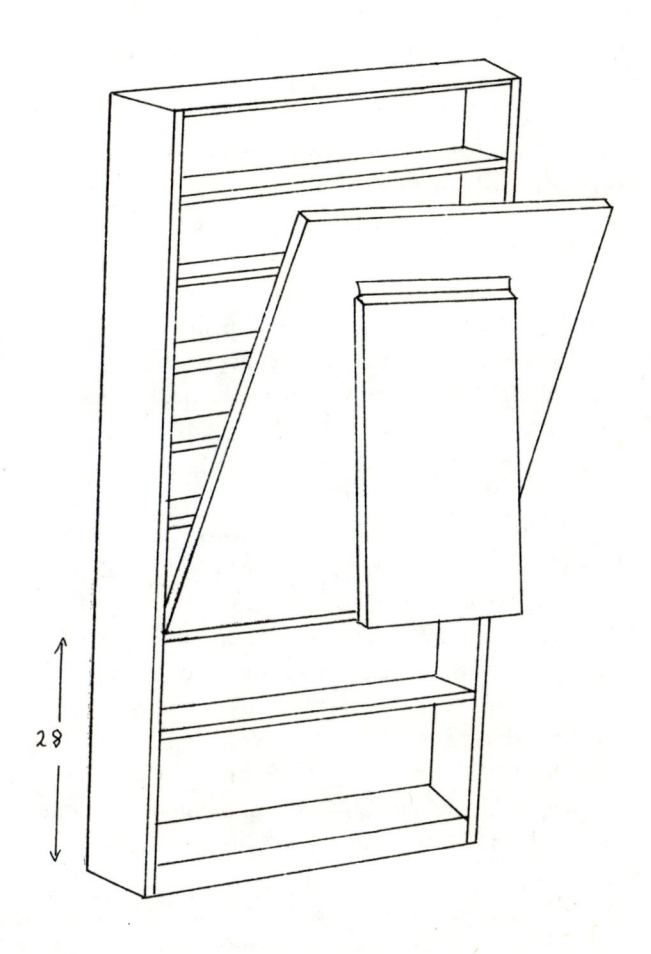

28

The table folds under the top shelf, but that's not necessary. It depends on the height and length of the bookcase and what space you want the table to fill when it's folded. The leg section can be used to hang a picture, paint a mural, or whatever, so that when it's

85

all folded up there's not a great expanse of wood. The table is held in place to the top of the bookcase by a metal hook and eye at each side. The shelves behind the folded table can be used for books but would also be good for glasses and silverware, napkins, and other table paraphernalia.

The same principle of a table top extending from a bookcase also makes it easy to build a desk. It's not a surface you'd want to lift up or fold most of the time, but it's easy enough to attach one end of the desk *on* a shelf in the bookcase while the other end can be supported by boxes in which you can put shelves for stationery and office or artists' supplies.

One of the cheapest table, desk, or even bed, surfaces it's possible to buy is a smooth, unfinished, hollow, wooden door. You can buy them at lumberyards or special house fixture supply stores for about $12. At this price, you get plain old pine; if you're prepared to pay more and want a different surface, the price of the door will naturally increase in price with the quality of the wood. If you're lucky, you can find an old door on a building site or when someone else is putting new doors in their home.

The standard door size is 8′ long x 3′ wide. If 8′ is too long for the space you've designated for it, the store or lumberyard will generally cut it down to size for you, reblock the end (because the door actually is hollow), and charge you a few dollars for it.

Plywood would work just as well for the desk surface, but there's not much difference in price, and there's something particularly solid looking and craftsmanlike about the door.

A good desk height is, as with tables, 28″. A couple of inches either way doesn't matter—it depends on what's comfortable for you. The height of my desk is 28″, and fortunately one of the shelves in the bookcase was almost 27″ high. The desk top itself is $1\frac{1}{2}″$ thick, and the surface height from the floor a shade over the 28″. Orange crates, however, are only 24″, and they were built up to the proper height with a base made from scraps of wood from another box in exactly the same way as the Totem base.

The shelves in the orange crate filing/stationery cupboard are just $\frac{1}{4}″$ plywood pieces resting on 1 x 1 wooden support strips. The inside dimensions of the orange crate are $22\frac{1}{4}″$ x $12\frac{3}{4}″$ x $12\frac{3}{4}″$ and the shelves themselves 22″ x $12\frac{1}{2}″$ wide x $12\frac{1}{2}″$ deep—just a shade narrower so that I can pull them out of the box easily and reach for things on them. The 1 x 1s are glued to the sides of the orange crate about every 3″ and then nailed with brads through the box and into the supports.

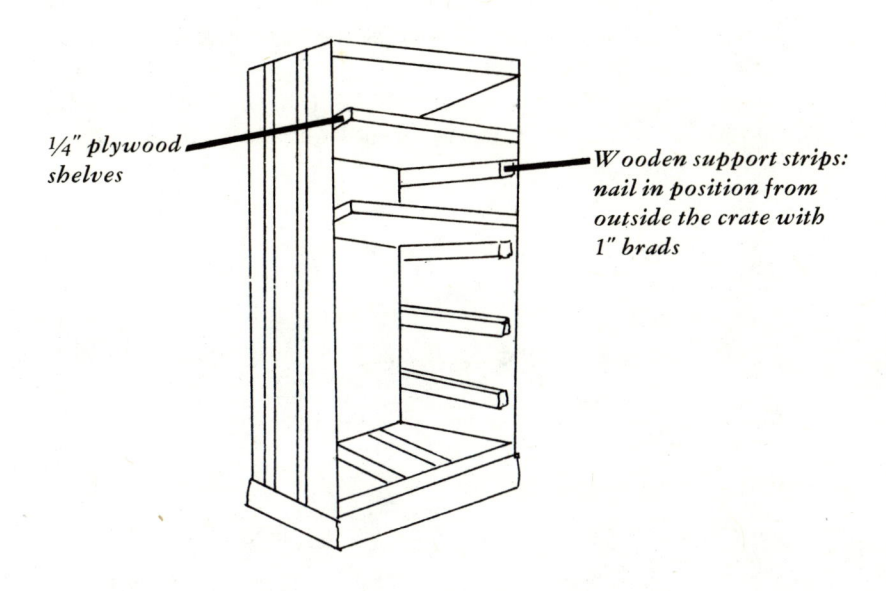

¼″ plywood shelves

Wooden support strips: nail in position from outside the crate with 1″ brads

If you don't want to support one end of the desk on a bookshelf, you can rest the whole thing on orange crates or other boxes. There's no reason to be confined to any of these suggestions —they're all adaptable for other combinations, and hopefully they'll suggest other possibilities. So much of it depends on your own apartment and your own needs.

A box can be a table—an end table, a coffee table—without doing anything more complicated than putting it in position beside a chair. A very simple, distinctive, table can be built with an orange crate and a sheet of glass. It doesn't have to be an orange crate, but boxes with slats, rather than solid wood, work well for this particular table: There's a certain freedom, and you can see inside the box. All you do is place the crate on the floor with the open end facing up. Around the inside edge of the crate, recessed about $\frac{1}{2}''$, attach strips of flat molding.

Have a piece of glass cut to the exact inside dimensions of the edges of the crate and drop it, gently, on to the molding. And you have a glass-topped coffee table.

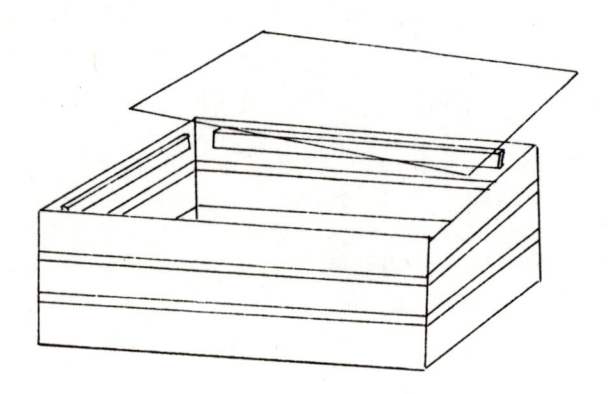

Underneath the glass, inside the box, a green plant, or a lamp, or a figurine or whatever you like will look good. If you want a larger coffee table, use two or three crates together. The crates can be stained or painted, or perhaps stained on the outside and painted on the inside.

Next to turning a box upside-down and using the bottom of it as a table top, the simplest table is one which is a sheet of $\frac{3}{4}''$ plywood, cut to whatever size you want, and placed on boxes, either at each end or in the center. The boxes can be used for storage, with or without doors.

THINGS
TO BUILD
AND HOW

Another table, easy to make and easy to take apart, is made with the same $\frac{3}{4}''$ plywood top and a "cross-over" base, also cut from $\frac{3}{4}''$ plywood.

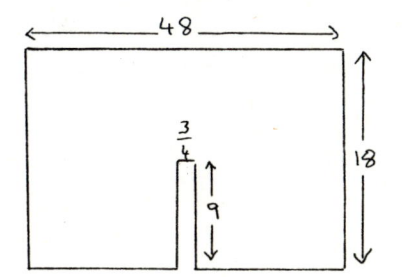

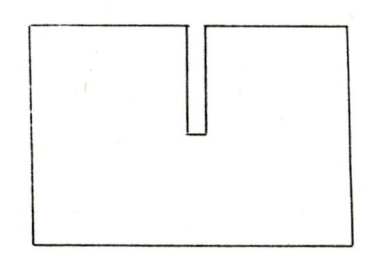

For a 36" square coffee table, or even a dining table, you'll need three pieces of $\frac{3}{4}''$ plywood: one 36" x 36" piece for the top and two pieces for the base, cut as follows:

The two base pieces slot into each other forming a solid cruciform unit. Even without gluing the two pieces together, the base will be pretty steady and solid. The diagonal length of a 36" square table top is slightly over 54" (54.414"). The base is cut in two 48" lengths, which allows 3" in from each corner of the table top. The height is flexible, depending on what you want and where you want to use the table.

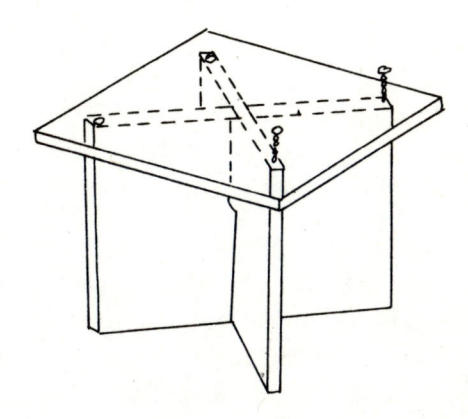

89

The table top should be glued and screwed into the base. Put the screws in so that they are set slightly below the surface of the table top; the heads can be covered with wood putty. When the whole is sanded and finished, the screws won't show.

The same design can, by the way, be applied to stools. Because the seating area will be smaller than the table top the base of the stool should be as wide as the seat. Otherwise it might not be sturdy enough.

Children and Boxes

As large as life and twice as natural
LEWIS CARROLL, *Through the Looking Glass*

IT'S TRUE, I haven't had much to do with children—some friends have them, and I see them around on buses—but from what little I've seen, they need sturdy, colorful, movable furniture; things to knock over, climb under, and hide their belongings in. Box furniture, perhaps, really comes into its own with children. Boxes are built to their size, and very little work is needed in putting things together for them.

A child's table is a simple matter of two boxes and a piece of plywood. Storage is created the same way on top of the table, if you like.

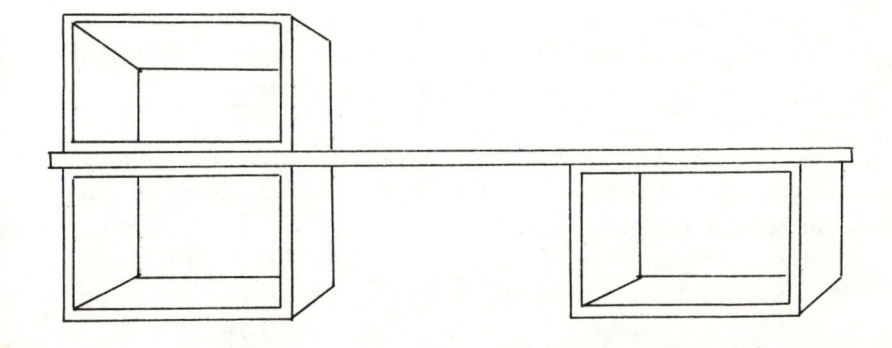

When the child grows taller, the boxes can be turned around and shelves added to them.

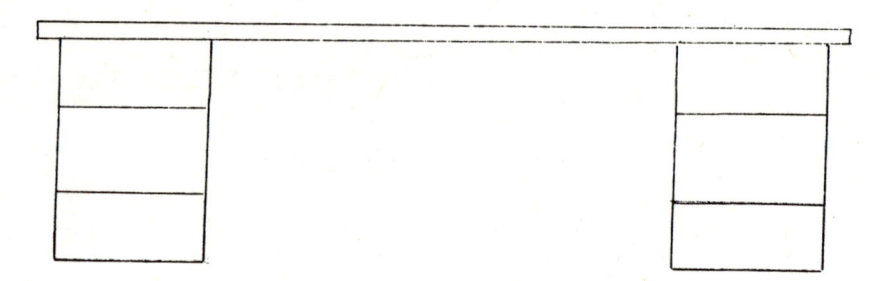

Another box, with a cushion, is an easy stool.

Boxes painted in different, but solid, colors to hold toys can be stacked against a wall or in a square in the middle of the room. Doors can be added to some of them. The whole unit can be expanded and heightened as the children grow and accumulate more junk. The boxes should be stacked so that the children can reach them—in other words, not too high and not awkwardly.

Everything already suggested in this book can be adapted for use by children—a bed, something to sit on, a place to put things, a surface to work on. What more do any of us want? Children are no different, just learning.

From what I see of children, they like places to look in, are fascinated by colors and doors, things they can move around all by themselves. A child's room is one place where boxes should be painted, rather than varnished to adult tastes.

CHILDREN
AND BOXES

Boxes make great toys. A tea chest can become a maze if you cut climbable-through holes in the sides, so that the children can chase each other through and around and over. Several tea chests must be heaven.

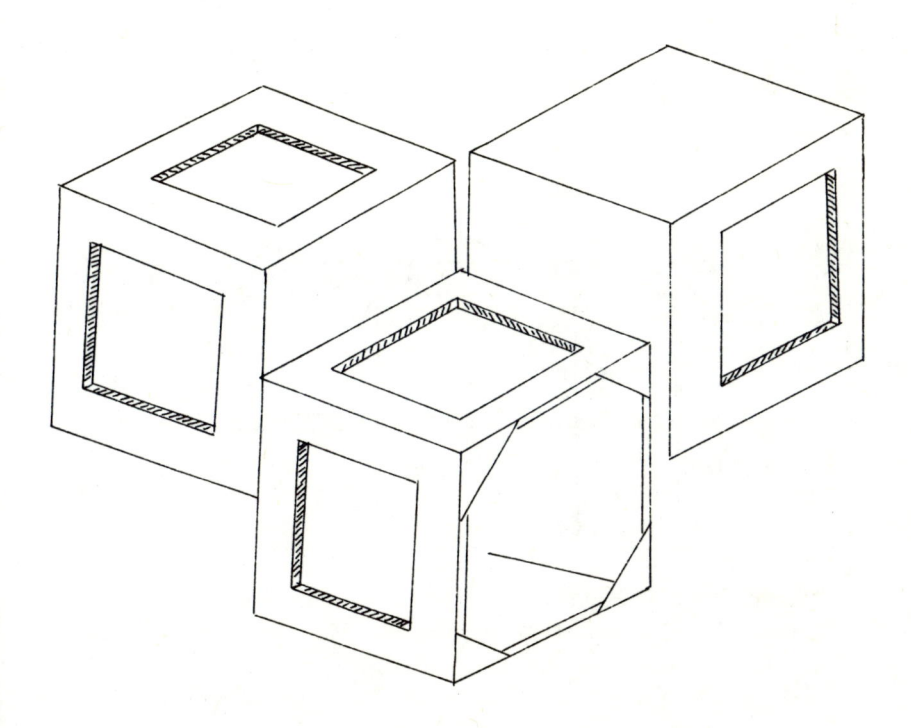

Small cardboard or wood boxes can be used as building blocks, either all the same size or ones that fit inside each other. The corners can be strengthened with masking or scotch tape and the whole box painted in bright colors.

THE BOX BOOK

Children like to carry bags and boxes around with them, to move their treasures along with them. A cigar box or something slightly larger is perfect. Put different compartments inside the box and little doors on the side of the box which open into the different compartments. A handle on top and the box makes it a magic suitcase.

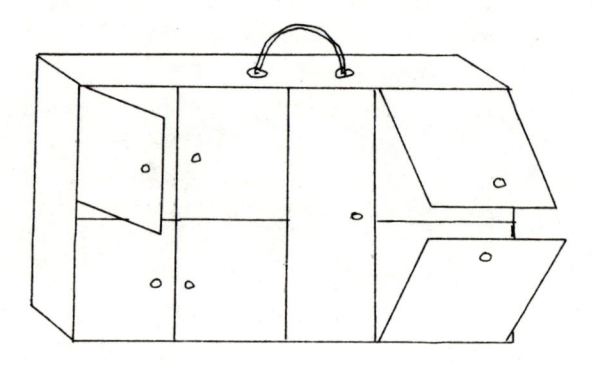

Actually, there's no need to go to even this trouble. Put a child in a room full of boxes, leave him alone, and see what happens. Children know exactly what they need and what they want at any given time. They'll arrange it all themselves and be happy doing it.

Pure Folly

*How sad and mad and bad it was
But then, how it was sweet!*
BROWNING, *Confessions*

ONE OF THE things that happens when you build your own furniture is that you become very fond of it—unreasonably so at times. It's a fondness mixed with amusement at the idea of having put all this funny furniture together from old boxes and plywood, furniture that in some amazing way really does work and looks good.

In the 18th and 19th centuries the British had a penchant for what they called "follies," wonderful, elaborate structures built without obvious purpose—a full-size replica of the Coliseum in a garden, a purposefully ruined tower atop a hill, an arch leading nowhere, a Gothic façade to a modest cottage. The purpose of a folly is delight in the ridiculous; pleasure in building, designing, and amusing. The most famous folly in America is Simon Rodea's Towers in Watts, California. Rodea spent his life scouring garbage dumps and building sites, putting his discoveries—bricks and rocks, glass, and household junk—into elaborate structures rising high into the sky. They're magic and wonderful and built purely for his own delight, and, as a by-product, ours, too.

A friend with a greater sense of whimsy than I decided that my apartment lacked a liquor cabinet and that the only place left for anything might be the small area between the bathroom door and the end of a built-in bookcase. It's an area 7′2″ high x 16″ wide x 9″ deep. Plum crates, mirrors, four wooden legs, and the thought led to a folly called Wunderbar.

The idea was to build something as fanciful as possible in the confines of space and materials we had, keeping in mind at all times the elaborateness of commercial liquor cabinets—pink lights, plus interiors, and a music box at its core which bursts forth with "Drink To Me Only" when the doors are opened.

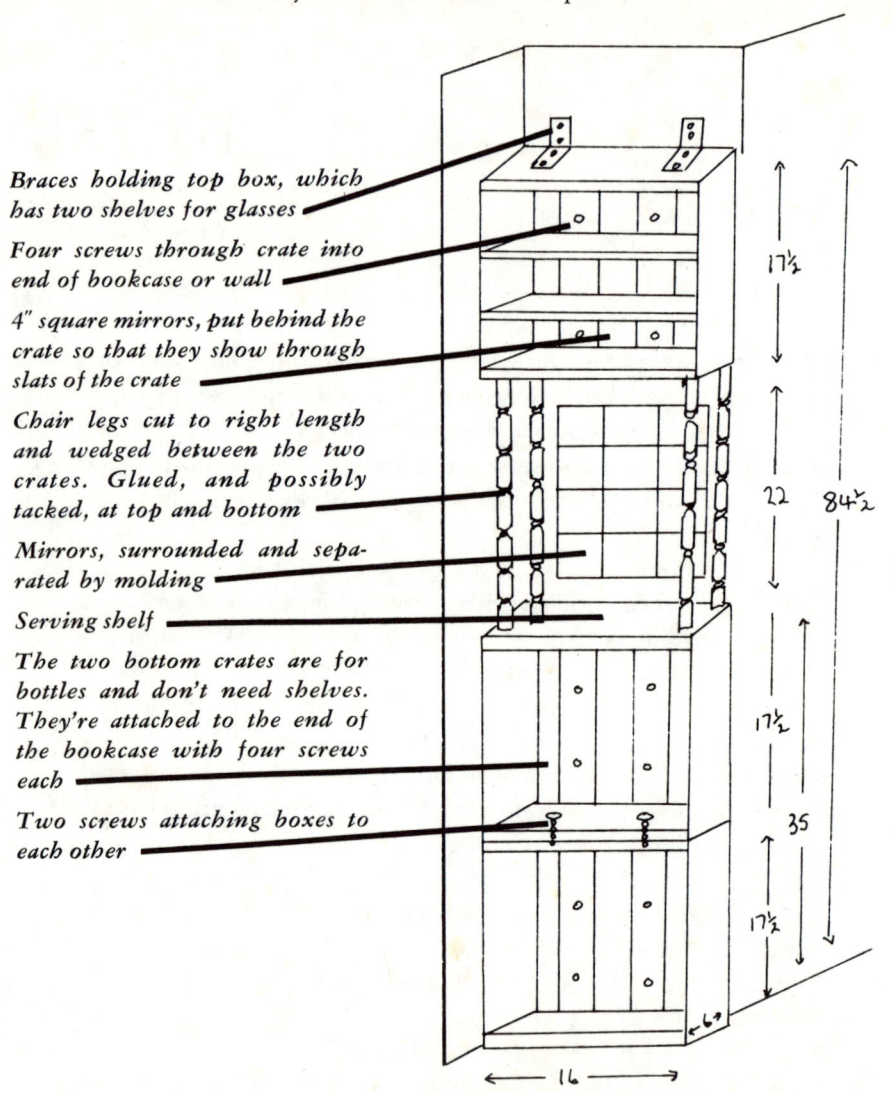

Braces holding top box, which has two shelves for glasses

Four screws through crate into end of bookcase or wall

4" square mirrors, put behind the crate so that they show through slats of the crate

Chair legs cut to right length and wedged between the two crates. Glued, and possibly tacked, at top and bottom

Mirrors, surrounded and separated by molding

Serving shelf

The two bottom crates are for bottles and don't need shelves. They're attached to the end of the bookcase with four screws each

Two screws attaching boxes to each other

You may not need a liquor cabinet, but you might have an odd space that wouldn't be lost by putting some structure in it and using it for some kind of storage. Also, you might not fancy a folly in your apartment, or perhaps not the same kind of folly, but box furniture has a tendency to lead one in this direction.

What it takes to build this folly:

1) An awkward, narrow space.
2) Three plum crates 16" x 17½" x 6".
    (The type of crate and size is flexible depending on the boxes you can find and whether they'll fit your space).
3) Four legs, or a broom handle cut into four lengths, measuring 22" long.
4) Twelve 4" square mirrors. These can be bought in some lumberyards, hardware stores, and Five-and-Ten stores. They cost less than $3 for nine squares and come with self-adhesive pads for attaching to the wall.
5) 130" of decorative molding, ¼" wide.
6) Two braces for additional support of the top plum crate, fourteen 3/4" screws, two ½" screws, eight nails, four brads, glue.

1) The most time-consuming and complicated thing about Wunderbar is putting the 4" square mirrors in the right places on the bookcase behind the top plum crate, so that they show through the slats of the crate. The open space between each slat is 3½" wide; the mirror is 4", which means that ¼" of the mirror on each side will go underneath, and be hidden by, the edge of the slats on each side of it. The length of the space inside the box is 15½"—that's four mirrors down and ¼" above the top and below the bottom of the crate. To get the right placings, hold the top plum crate in position and mark with pencil the open areas where the mirrors will fall on the end of the bookcase or a wall. Then put the mirrors in position. The mirrors here are placed next to each other, not separated by the molding, as below.

2) The rest of it is very straightforward. The bottom crate is put in place and screwed to the end of the bookcase with four ¾" screws. The second crate is placed on top of that, screwed to the bookcase and, with two screws, into the crate it's resting on.

3) Then skip 22" of space and screw the top plum crate to the bookcase on top of the mirror squares already in position. For extra support, put two braces on top of the crate and into the bookcase. (The $\frac{1}{2}$" screws are used for attaching the brace to the box.) Before putting this crate in place, fix the shelves into it—$\frac{1}{2}$" plywood or wood taken from another crate. The best way of deciding on shelf heights is to measure the glasses you want to put on them and fix the shelves accordingly.

4) The central mirror, the focal point of Wunderbar, is made with sixteen 4" mirror squares, surrounded and separated by the $\frac{1}{4}$" decorative molding. Measure the outside dimensions of the full piece first—mirrors plus the width of each strip of molding (4" each mirror, $\frac{1}{4}$" each strip of molding). Three mirrors across (12"), plus four strips of molding at $\frac{1}{4}$" each come to a total width of 13". The total length is four mirrors down (16"), plus five strips of $\frac{1}{4}$" molding, making $17\frac{1}{4}$" altogether. Mark this out in pencil on the end of the bookcase or wall where you're building and glue the outside molding frame into position.

5) Put the first 4" square into the top left-hand corner of the frame. Underneath that, place the first piece of molding across the

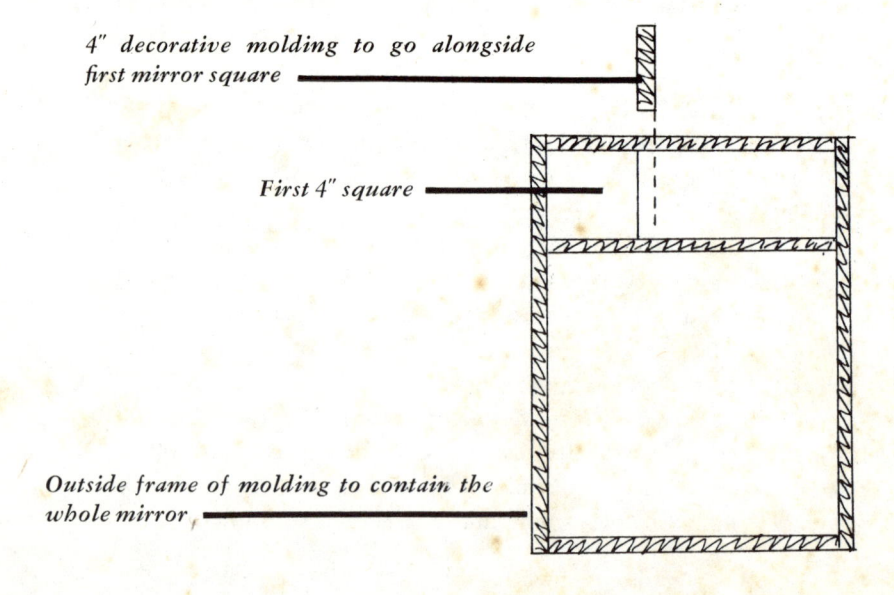

4" *decorative molding to go alongside first mirror square*

First 4" square

Outside frame of molding to contain the whole mirror

whole width of the mirror, which is 12½". The down strips of molding are cut to 4" lengths and placed alongside each mirror square as it's put in position. And so on through.

6) Finally, the legs go into position. They should be glued between the crates and, for extra strength, tacked into place with brads through the top and bottom shelves.

Now, looking at Wunderbar, I realize how lucky it was that my apartment had this built-in bookcase; it provided the perfect awkward space. You may not have a space quite like it, but you're bound to have an odd corner somewhere where something like this can be built. You could, of course, always create such a space.

Wunderbar pretends to be nothing more than a suggestion. It is, though, one of my favorite things, falling into that definition of a folly—a structure without obvious purpose.

Some Odds and Ends and Decorative Things

> All sorts of things and weather
> Must be taken in together
> To make up a year
> And a sphere
> RALPH WALDO EMERSON, *Fable: The Mountain and the Squirrel*

YOU MIGHT, AT this point, think my apartment looks as if it's furnished with boxes. Not so, at least at first glance. If the boxes are integrated as furniture, changed by the environment of your apartment, they really do become couches and cupboards and anything else you decide they should.

Once you launch into building things from boxes, their applications become endless. It's hard to walk down the street without finding a wooden box. It's even harder to walk past that box, even though your apartment may be jammed solid with box furniture. The chances are you won't walk past it. In fact, two months ago you scoured the neighborhood looking for one just like it, so you'll take it home and stack it somewhere until you can decide exactly what to do with it.

There are several boxes in my apartment waiting for something to be done with them. Eventually, they'll be absorbed; they always are. Some of the boxes I've hoarded have worked their way into very useful things.

One of these odd objects is a stool (below) made from a Greek crate (probably used to carry grapes). It's $13\frac{1}{2}''$ wide x $11\frac{1}{2}''$ high x $12\frac{1}{4}''$ deep. With the addition of a seat, which also works as a lid, it became a stool and storage space for newspapers. The lid was a scrap of wood found on the street and cut to size to fit the box. The cushion is a piece of foam rubber covered in burlap.

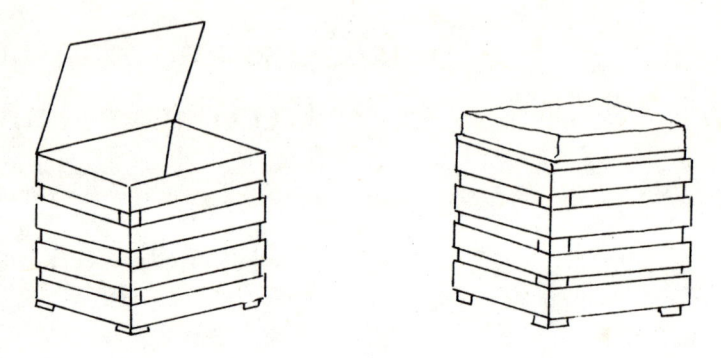

A wine crate seemed a natural file cabinet (below). It lacked a top, but $\frac{1}{2}''$ plywood cut to size worked fine. Actually, the top of the wine crate became the side of the file cabinet, and the side became a lid. Brass fittings, a handle, hinges, and a hasp made it easy to close and carry around.

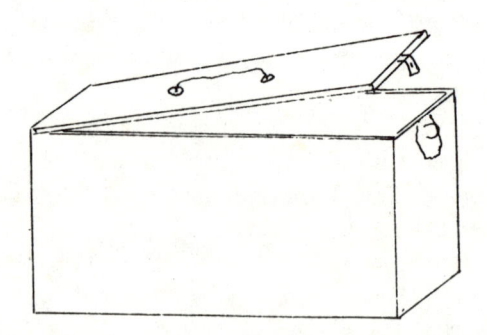

ODDS AND
ENDS AND
DECORATIVE
THINGS

Asparagus boxes from California can present a problem. They're awkwardly shaped for most purposes (other than carrying asparagus), but the one I have worked its way into a shoe-shine box:

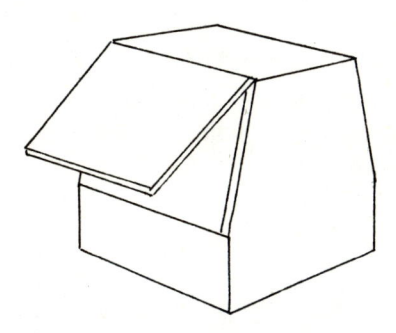

Without doing a thing to them, Coca Cola and Pepsi Cola boxes are great. They're shallow boxes divided into square compartments for bottles. You could continue to put bottles in it by making a wine rack from it, but these boxes make good wall decorations, too. You can paint them different colors (they come in red and yellow), hang them on a wall, and put little things in the different compartments. They're also useful on top of desks for small odds and ends that accumulate, and cry out for pigeon holes:

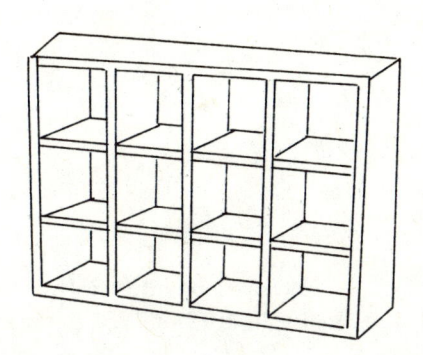

One of the best boxes I have was found by a friend on a New York pier. I don't know where it comes from or what came in it, but it's 20" x 15" x 14", has recessed sides, and is smooth and fresh-smelling inside. First of all, it was stained, then the top and sides tiled with ceramic tiles from Spain. Tiles aren't terribly expensive and can be used effectively on table tops, chests, and shelves. To fix them in place, use something called grout, which comes in packages, is mixed with water, and works into a consistency much like plaster. The pier box, which became a linen chest (below), already had recessed sides into which the tiles fit easily. It didn't need much building up to make the tiles and the top of the box flush.

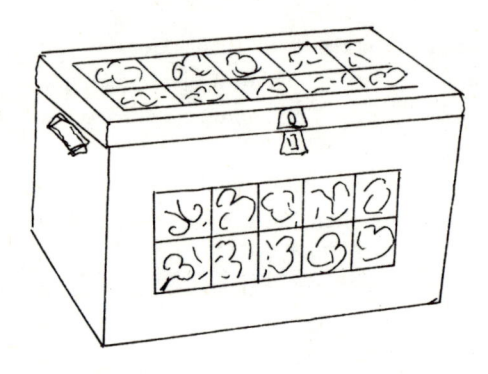

If you wanted to tile a surface into which standard size tiles didn't fit evenly—standard is 2", 3", 4" and 6" square—you could

ODDS AND ENDS AND DECORATIVE THINGS

either cut the tiles or use fewer tiles and surround them with wood molding, building the surface out to the edges. This will create a frame for the tiles. To make the edges of the surface and the tiles look as if they belong to each other place a molding around the edges of the surface.

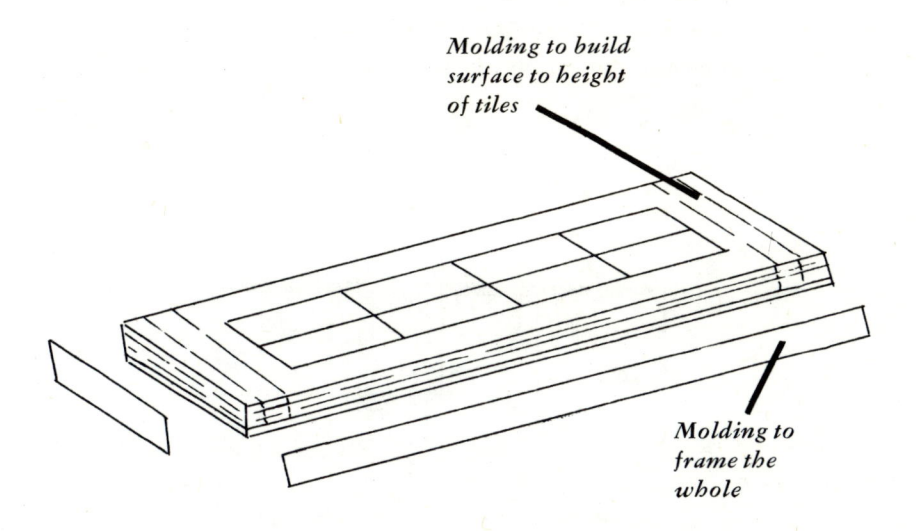

Molding to build surface to height of tiles

Molding to frame the whole

Tiles are also a way to frame mirrors. The best way to do that is decide what size you want first, buy the tiles, work them into a frame and then get the mirror cut to the right size. It's best to use $\frac{1}{2}''$ plywood as backing for the whole thing—$\frac{1}{4}''$ wouldn't be strong enough to hold the tiles and the mirror.

Printers keep their different type faces in cabinets known as California job cases. Look out for one of these or find an old printing house or a place that sells secondhand printing equipment and ask if they have a job case you can buy. The case is divided into 102 small compartments. (Each is for a different letter of the alphabet, commas, semi-colons, and so on). Hang the case on a wall and put small things you like to look at into each of the compartments—shells, stamps, buttons, anything small that fits. Don't do anything to the case but clean it. It doesn't need any help in looking good and it should be shown off in its original state.

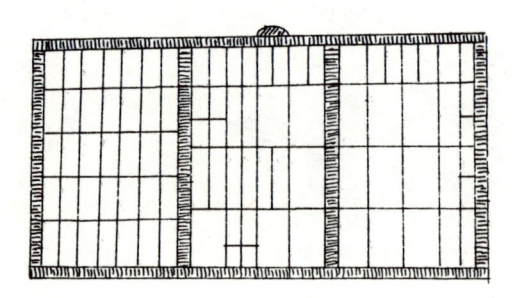

Lighting fixtures can be expensive, but not if you make them. The electrical fittings you need to make a lamp are inexpensive and should be bought, but the bases and shades can be made cheaply and can make the difference between practical lighting and decorative lighting. We all know about bottles as lamps, but it doesn't have to be an old green bottle. There are some wonderfully shaped and decorated clear bottles in all shapes and sizes, and they can be filled with sand or small shells or pebbles.

There are lots of things around to find which can be worked into lamps very effectively and inexpensively. Some of the odd pieces of wood left over from some of the furniture can be built into a sculpture which can become a lamp. I have a piece of copper tubing which I fixed into a scrap of wood to make a lamp base. The shade is made from a biscuit tin, painted red. (Some Mexican lamps I've seen are made from tin.) A similar hanging lamp can be made from an empty coffee can.

Reflective lighting can be produced very inexpensively by buying spot lights (about $2) from hardware stores. They come with clamps and can be put on bookshelves with the light directed toward a wall or the ceiling. The light bounces back and gives a soft white light. The $2 lights aren't exactly attractive, but they can be painted different colors. If you decide to do this, you should ask at the hardware store for a paint which will take the heat; ordinary gloss paint will smell and peel if it's exposed to too much heat.

Finishing Things Off

*Raise ye the stone or cleave the wood
To make a path more fair or flat*
RUDYARD KIPLING, *The Song of Martina*

NOW THAT YOU'VE made all this furniture, it needs to be finished, not only because finishing brings out the good qualities of the wood and shows off the piece of furniture to full advantage, but because the object needs some protection from dirt and stains. There are all kinds of finishes—stains, lacquers, enamel paints, oils, and waxes. The most effective for box and plywood furniture is colored varnish; it's easy to apply and looks the best with least work. Also, as all the furniture is made from boxes and plywood, the sturdiness of varnish will hide many of the faults in the wood. It will also prevent white rings made by heat or water from forming on table tops.

Colored varnish can be bought in hardware and Five-and-Ten stores in various wood shades—mahogany (which should be avoided, because it always ends up being too red), teak (a very light stain which doesn't have a terribly rich glow), light and dark oak (better, although both shades end up being rather grayish), and lots of others. The best shade I've found is walnut (either light or dark), and after early experimentation with other shades have used it for practically everything. The only thing to do is try them all out—and on boxes you can afford to. The boxes in the early furniture I built are all in different shades. It didn't matter too much if the odd box wasn't a glowing, rich color, and I wasn't interested in conformity of shades. (Every box in the totem, for example, is different.) On a large structure, though, when you want it to look like one piece, it can be disastrous if you varnish the whole thing mahogany and decide you don't like its redness. Try the varnish shades out on scraps of the same wood before launching into a major job.

Sanding

The first thing you do with any surface, whether it's a box, plywood, or pine, is to sand it down. Boxes are made of rough, cheap wood, and full of lurking splinters. Plywood, too, needs just as much sanding down. It might be cheap wood, but if it's finished off properly—and that means beginning with a good sanding—it can be made to look really fine.

Use a fine-grained sandpaper wrapped around a block of wood. (This makes it easier to handle and gives an even pressure.) The sandpaper should not be pushed and pulled across the grain of the wood—you'll end up with scratches. Instead, take it in the same direction as the grain. Working with the grain of the wood, by the way, applies to every process in finishing any piece of wood.

When you've sanded the surface down so that it feels smooth to the touch, clean all the particles of wood and dust off the surface. A wet sponge will do this, but make sure it's done thoroughly. If you don't, you'll end up with the dust in the varnish on the finished surface.

Shellac

Before varnishing (or staining), furniture needs a sealer to give a smoother finish to the whole thing. For boxes and plywood particularly, shellac is the best thing to use. It's brushed onto the surface of the wood, after it's sanded, to equalize the surface. Wood has soft and hard spots, and soft spots, without a sealer, would absorb the varnish more thoroughly than the hard spots and create an uneven-looking surface. Shellac will equalize the wood by going into the soft spots and hardening them. Then, when the varnish is applied, it will spread uniformly across the surface. If you don't do this you might end up with light, and dark and rough areas. This is particularly true of plywood and boxes but if the shellac base is applied first the varnish will go on evenly.

The shellac should be thinned first. Use one part shellac with one part denatured alcohol. It'll dry within about half an hour. And always buy small quantities of shellac, or whatever you need for a particular job, because it won't keep very well. It loses its sealer qualities and becomes sticky and difficult to handle.

When the shellac is dry, the surface should be sanded again, with a fine grade sandpaper.

Varnishing

Though sometimes frustrating, because it drips too easily or because you can see the brush marks, putting the varnish on is the best part. The varnish rolls out from your brush, transforming the rough piece of furniture into an object which glows and assumes its proper identity as a fine piece of craftsmanship. The cheap wood is hidden, the fine grain exposed.

Always use a new brush for varnishing. However well you think you've cleaned a brush, it will never apply the varnish as smoothly as a fresh brush. You can buy brushes for 60 or 70 cents, and it's worth the expense, because it will make a world of difference to the way the piece of furniture looks.

Never try to save old varnish—at least not more than a couple of weeks. It gets thick and lumpy and, even with thinning, won't work evenly. You should buy small cans of varnish, or as much as you need at any given time.

Although cans of color varnish do not suggest any thinning in their instructions, it goes on more evenly if you do. Add a small amount of mineral spirits to the varnish and mix it up well. Thinning the varnish makes it easier to work with and cuts down on the bubbles which form when varnish is first put on.

Before applying varnish to the surface make sure that it is free of dust by wiping thoroughly with a damp sponge.

Put the varnish on with short strokes and make sure the whole surface is covered. Some small bubbles will form, but don't worry about them—they will disintegrate and be absorbed as you continue working. After this initial covering, go over it again, smoothing the varnish out with longer strokes. Don't worry about brush marks either—they, too, will disappear as the varnish dries. Be careful on edges: The varnish will accumulate and drip over the edges down the sides. Just keep brushing the excess away and wiping the edges of the surface off with a cloth. Leave it all to dry.

When it is dry, go over the varnished surface with fine steel wool, this will give it a very smooth finished surface. At this point, you can either wax it, or, if you want an even deeper glow, give it another coat of varnish.

If you're varnishing a large area, watch out for the fumes which can give you an unbelievable headache and make you feel nauseated. Always try to work in a room with all the windows open and if possible don't hang around while it's drying. It's horrible stuff and can make you sick for days. Varnishing is the biggest disadvantage of working in a small apartment.

Often on plywood furniture—table top or chair—you'll want to put flat molding on its edges. This shouldn't be done until after the whole thing is stained. The molding should then be finished separately.

After all the varnishing is done is the time to add knobs and handles and other fixtures to cabinets and drawers. Never try to work around fixtures.

Of course, you could paint all the furniture in bright enamel paints, but it seems a shame to hide the wood that way. Sometimes—for considerations of space or design—enamel paint does look right, but wood has a texture that's worth preserving whenever possible.

One of the things I enjoy about boxes is the identifying lettering on the sides—names of companies, what was contained in the boxes, where they came from. Not all boxes have it, but when it's there, I let it shine through the varnish. I rather like the look of the lettering becoming part of the design; it's all part of the box.

The End

And that's all there is to it. Find the boxes and start building. The biggest effort of all is collecting boxes, but once you've notified local stores and friends that you want any wooden boxes they come across, you're halfway home. It's much harder to stop than to begin. My apartment has absorbed as many boxes as is possible, but still people are bringing them by, and still it's hard to resist any box I find on the streets. The time is obviously coming to move again, to take apart all the boxes, to pack them with my belongings, to move on to larger quarters, to more boxes and new assemblies.

Index

Asparagus boxes, 103

Bathroom, space saver, 24–26
Bookshelves, 74–80
   adjustable, 79
   ordering the backing, 78
   in sections, 75
Braces, 15
Brads, 13

Cabinet, 41–47
California job cases, 106
Chairs, 60–70
Child's room, 91–94
Chinese boxes, 4
Coca Cola boxes, 103
Cockroaches, getting rid of, 20
Coffee-can cabinet, 21–22
Common nails, 13
Contact cement, 8, 17
Couches, 56–59
Cupboards, 35–38

Door handles, 16
Drambuie and wine crates, 3
Drawer pulls, 16
Drawers, 51–53
Drill, 6–7

Epoxy glue, 8–9, 17

Fabrics, kinds of, 71
Finishing, 109–112
   sandpaper, 110
   shellac, 110–111
   varnish, 111–112
Finishing nails, driving, 14
Fixtures, 16
Follies, 95–99
   liquor cabinet, 96–99
   purpose of, 95

Garbage pail, 22–23
Glue, 17
Grape box, 3

Hammer, 5–6
Hardboard, 13
Hinges, 16

Kitchen, space saver, 20–24
Knobs, 16
Knotty pine, 12

Lamps, 106–107
Legs, 17
Lettering on the sides, 112
Lighting fixtures, 106–107

Milk crates, 2
Mirrors, tile framing, 105
Moldings, 12

Nail, how to, 13–14
Nails, types of, 13

Odds and ends, 101–107
Orange crates, 1

Pegboard, 23–24
Pepsi Cola boxes, 103
Pine, 12
Pliers, 7
Plum crates, 2
Plywood, grades and thicknesses, 11–12
Printers' cases, 106

Reflective lighting, 107

Sandpaper, using, 110
Saws, 8
Scotch tape, 17
Scraper, 8
Screwdriver, 7
Screws, 14–15
Seat covers, how to make, 71–73
Shellac, how to apply, 110–111
Shoe-shine box, 103
Space savers, 19–26
   bathroom, 24–26
   kitchen, 20–24
Standard bookshelf sizes, 12
Stool and storage space for newspapers, 101–103
Supports, brace, 15

Tables, 81–90
   for children, 91–92
Tape measure, 9

113

INDEX

Tea chests, 4
Things to build, 27–90
  bookshelves, 74–80
  cabinet, 41–47
  chairs, 60–75
  couches, 56–59
  drawers, 51–53
  seat covers, 71–73
  tables, 81–90
  totem, 27–34
  wall unit, 39–40, 48–50
Tiles, 104–105
Tools, 5–9
  drill, 6–7
  hammer, 5–6
  miscellaneous, 8–9
  pliers, 7
  saws, 8
  scraper, 8
  screwdriver, 7
Totem, 27–34

Varnish, how to apply, 111–112

Wall unit, 39–40, 48–50
  finishing, 54–55
Wine crates, 3
Wood putty, 18
Wooden boxes, kinds of, 1–4